The After Journey

Getting Through the First Year

Laurie-Ann Weis

TRAFFORD
PUBLISHING

Note for Librarians: A cataloguing record for this book is available from Library and Archives Canada at www.collectionscanada.ca/amicus/index-e.html
ISBN 1-4120-6670-0

Offices in Canada, USA, Ireland and UK
This book was published *on-demand* in cooperation with Trafford Publishing. On-demand publishing is a unique process and service of making a book available for retail sale to the public taking advantage of on-demand manufacturing and Internet marketing. On-demand publishing includes promotions, retail sales, manufacturing, order fulfilment, accounting and collecting royalties on behalf of the author.

Book sales for North America and international:
Trafford Publishing, 6E–2333 Government St.,
Victoria, BC v8t 4p4 CANADA
phone 250 383 6864 (toll-free 1 888 232 4444)
fax 250 383 6804; email to orders@trafford.com
Book sales in Europe:
Trafford Publishing (uk) Ltd., Enterprise House, Wistaston Road Business Centre,
Wistaston Road, Crewe, Cheshire cw2 7rp UNITED KINGDOM
phone 01270 251 396 (local rate 0845 230 9601)
facsimile 01270 254 983; orders.uk@trafford.com
Order online at:
trafford.com/05-1581

10 9 8 7 6 5 4 3

Dedication

To Steve, my late husband, who taught me what courage and passion truly mean. Thank you for making my life filled with unconditional love.

To Sadie Simms, my mother, who is my greatest role model. Your values and love have given me the ability to keep going when things get tough. Thank you for all of your unconditional love.

To Hy Simms, my stepfather, who always believed in me and made me feel so special. Thank you for being at every treatment, for opening up your heart and home to Steve. Thank you for watching over me from Heaven. I feel your spirit every day.

To Murray Granard, my biological father, who gave hours of time driving us everywhere and always had a positive attitude.

To All Caregivers and their loved ones; to all widows, widowers and partners; to all those who have lost a great love; and to all who are or have gone through this very difficult journey.

Acknowledgments

$\mathcal{A}$ special thank you to all of my website e-mail friends from many countries who have written letters to me opening up their hearts and souls with their most personal feelings and allowing me to learn that grief the first year is the same all over the world no matter race, religion, age or gender.

I wish to express my deep affection, appreciation, admiration and profound gratitude to Kristin Loberg, who became more than a skilled editor on a project but a friend who could finish my sentences, reliving and feeling this journey with me every step of the way. Without you, there would not be either book.

I wish to thank Roger Gittines for encouraging me at the beginning of this writing journey to dig deep and write the truth.

I wish to thank everyone who worked at Reliance Steel and Aluminum who allowed Steve to continue to work with dignity and grace and continued to be gracious to me after his death.

I would like to pay tribute to my friends and family who have given freely and differently with their love, time and patience: Paul Abell, Rochelle and Mike Milmeister, Don and Madeline Karpel, Kathy and Barry Fiedel, Yvonne, Nate and Nicole Matilsky, Oscar Jimenez, The Mann Family (Larry, Gloria, Danny, Ron, Ginger, Ricky and Jeff), Jill Wolff, Kathy Porterfield., Robyn Rakov, Christine Shook, Donna Held, Sheila and Tony Sauber, Bobbi Sloan, Sylvia Hill, Aaron Doty, Ben Posen, Martha Maley, Jennifer Deshaies, Gerry Bloch, Jimmy Marshall, Tom Harkenrider, Michael (the neighba) Stephens, Rick Butler, Angelo, Chrisa and Dino Takos, Debbie and Steve Kaner, Franck and Tania Kalenga, Nancy Madey, Nancy Perrin, Lisa Peter Family, Roy Pruneda, Tom and Mike Aizawa.

I would like to thank Dr. Tony King, who taught me to "ride the horse" and still continues to guide me when I am stuck or begin to fall off.

To Pete Egoscue, who believed in me and my future when I couldn't, I humbly acknowledge the wisdom you have shared with me over the years.

To Dr. Ken Rexinger and staff, who were always available and gave us support for anything and everything and still continue to support my needs, I truly thank you with so much appreciation.

To Dr. Manuel Fernandez who continues to listen and guide me without judgment, I thank you and deeply respect your opinions.

A gigantic thank you to Dr. Judith Ford, Dr. Lee Rosen, Dr. Tim Solberg, Gage Daigle, nurses, technicians and receptionists at UCLA who treated us like we mattered.

A warm thank you to Steve's personal nurses who took great care of our family and made things as normal as possible.

A special thank you to all of my students and their parents for their unwavering support. A special acknowledgement to Jessica, Kristina, Philip, Nick and Natalie.

To Darin Mc Coy, who is a magician with my computer, a huge acknowledgment and appreciation for your skills and patience.

With appreciation to Doug Anderson and Gina Fiedel who allowed my creative process to grow with the website. You are so patient and kind.

To my neighbors, who make me smile and play a significant role in my life. I thank you for your greetings and conversation each day.

Thank you to Rebecca and Nyla for great communication and sharing your thoughts. You are both so inspiring.

To Sheila Ellison, for her compassion and willingness to contact others in support of my project. I think you are a gift and I thank you.

I would like to thank Terre Britton whose gentleness, enthusiastic support and creativity brought color to the project.

With gratitude and appreciation to Oprah Winfrey, a mentor I have never personally met but whose influence through her television show helped me to find my way back to my spirituality. Thank you for introducing me to Gary Zukav's teachings, which helped me find meaning and purpose in my life again without anger.

A special thank you to Chaplin Howard Young for his words, "Listening to your life is where self care begins."

And to my "Precious Treasure," thank you. Words cannot express my deepest appreciation for your emotional support concerning my needs and my dreams. Your words and love give me strength and balance and you raise the bar of joy in my life.

"We must reinvent ourselves and our lives to find a 'new normal' with a different joy."

To The Reader

$\mathcal{A}$ potential publisher once said to me that the stories in this book were self indulgent. She meant it as a harsh criticism, not realizing that she missed the point of *The After Journey*—a book that incorporates the experiences of new widows and widowers during their first year after a great loss.

This motivated me even more to publish this book because the first step as a widow or widower is to be self indulgent. Or, as I prefer to say it, uniquely focused on the self. This is the logical consequence for having been selfless during the extreme care of a sick and dying loved one, or for losing a loved one in a shocking moment. We not only lose the partner but we lose ourselves, which forces us to then practice extreme self care in order to reinvent ourselves and our life.

Being self indulgent to a degree is a necessary part of finding a way out of grief. Knowing others have gone through this self indulgent time gives grievers strength because they get to see that they, too, will come out of it and they are normal going through it. This will be evident to you as you read the stories from beginning to end.

Table of Contents

Introduction

The first year after the loss of a partner holds many new experiences—whether you were married by law or not. Even though I had supportive people in my life, I trudged through that first year feeling empty, scared, devastated, angry...and alone.

I wasn't one of those people who had the strength to attend a bereavement group. I was in shock with too much physical and emotional pain. My husband's death knocked the very breath out of my heart and soul.

I grew up influenced by television shows like "Leave It to Beaver" and "Father Knows Best." I knew that I would follow in those footsteps with a husband, children, grandchildren and a lot of friends. I also knew I'd attend college and have a career of my own. Although I didn't grow up like Cinderella, I dreamt about marrying my prince. And I did. I found him after one young marriage, and a few personal tragedies. We married when I was thirty-six years old. After 13 magnificent but short years, cancer took him.

I never thought about being widowed or rearing a child alone. I never thought about being single again. I believed that Steve and I would grow old together. My friends were all happily married. No one spoke about death. It wasn't a topic discussed. It happened in the movies and it happened to someone else. Surprise! It happened to me.

I wish I had this book during that first year as a widow. This isn't written by a doctor, a spiritual leader, or a philosopher. This book is written by someone who lost joy and the reason to wake up every morning. I had been evicted out of my world and thrown into an altered state of consciousness. A foreign land I had never traveled before. No map. No guiding light. No breadcrumbs to mark my path. *This is normal*, I kept telling myself per the advice of others. But I didn't believe it. Nothing about my life and my loss felt normal. What's normal? Everything was so alien to my being that not even abnormal could define me. I was lost. A few new people entered my life during this time who made tremendous impacts on my healing—strangers who helped without knowing it. I could deal with new people because they knew nothing about me and my past; they didn't conjure the face of Steve or rankle the shackles of the tragedy the way my friends and family could. I searched for a new support group separate from the one that carried me through to the funeral. Eventually, little by little, I learned how to push sadness aside and open my spirit back up to joy.

Bad things happen to good people. This I know for sure. I've journeyed far on my own and learned a lot since that eighth day of January when my love story ended. For a long time, I went to bed at night wishing for another visit from my husband in a magical dream so I could see him and hear his voice. Sometimes I took sleeping pills to get through the dark of night; the pills would put a leash on my brain, making it stop thinking so hard, calculating the sorrow and reliving the horror. My thoughts were hard to stop. My mind kept going, the pain kept churning. So long as my heart kept beating in my chest and I remained bound by Earth's clock, I was stuck with my thoughts. No matter where I went, I took myself with me—memories, emotions, God and all.

Aloneness is not a prison. Neither is it the same thing

as loneliness, although that does come to play a big part in being alone. Loneliness is an emotion, while aloneness is a state of being that befriends myriad emotions, many of them good ones. The other side of broken is knowing that you are not necessarily the princess with prince charming living in the castle…but knowing that you can live alone and not be empty. Life takes things away that you thought you couldn't live without and you always dreamed you needed; but life also makes exchanges, giving you different things of joy if you do the work to find them. Taking long walks by the sea, laughing with a friend, meeting new people, becoming transfixed by a match point in a tennis match—these are all things that bring you joy again if you allow them to. Food begins to taste good again, your sex drive returns, music invigorates you instead of making you cry, and your body feels alive once again. A new body, that is. Then, when you work at recognizing your bad feelings and reframing your thoughts for a few seconds, those seconds and those bad feelings begin to subside. The good begins to come in like a cool breeze.

Death doesn't take our capacity to love and to find that joy again, but the joy will be different. Joy is the absence of pain. If there's one thing death is good for, it certainly clarifies the fragility of life and shows us that we must live each day well. To do otherwise is to fail ourselves and those who have gone before us because they gave their energy so that we could continue to live and live well. It's no different than parents putting energy into their children. If we don't live our life well, it's an insult—a betrayal to the intention of their legacy.

Life after the death of a loved one is never the same again. It's hard to believe, but you can find joy and it's inside yourself. Joy is always there, somewhere. It lives within all of us, hidden within our veins and crouching behind the curtains of our daily grinds. You just have to recognize it.

You just have to seize it; get it to come out and help fight the daily battles. Joy won't present itself on its own. Lend it a hand and it might surprise you, make you laugh and smile like you did "back then." I hope this book helps you discover joy again in its new face, so that you can slowly regain the strength to go on living.

When the World Trade Center smoked and collapsed with lives, journeys, promises, security, and thousands of what-might-have-beens, I was there, in many ways, with those people left behind. And I still am. The smoke eventually clears, but the world underneath is never the same again. Lives change, people grapple with the weight of an irreconcilable sadness for the rest of their lives. It's hard to transcend tragedy; it's hard to find purpose in life again for yourself and trust that things will work out for the best. I've had to reframe how I see the world and my place in it. So have a lot of people.

I tried to write during that first year I was alone. Someone had suggested that I write my feelings and emotions down—that I keep a journal of my journey forward. But I was too numb to do that and I didn't do the grief journal well. Every time I tried to sit down and write my thoughts onto paper, I started to cry and shake, making a mess of things. Nothing could hold my attention, not the TV, a book, or a movie. Music, on the other hand, absorbed me completely. I had different songs for different moods, and kept the music playing whether I was walking, lying on my bed or sitting in the garden. The music would play forward while my mind would cast backward, reminiscing all the days of happiness gone.

Sometimes I cannot believe that I am still here in this world, that I am still living, breathing and watching the sun curl around the sky and set over the ocean every day. I know that I am not alone in mourning, for people die every day and leave loved ones behind. Death is one of those sure things in life. But coping with death is a very personal experience—something no other person can share in exactly the same way. Pain and grief becomes you. Pain takes on a force so ferocious as to take hold of you, shake you and never let you go. Until you accept pain as an emotion to manage, as you would anger, frustration and anxiety, it remains a sword. The sword is sharpest during that first year alone and remains stabbing our hearts the second year as the numbness wears off and reality sets in. Steve died six years ago, and I still have my moments. I have to remind myself that my lessons are not over yet.

The motivation for writing this book originated from a Web site I started more than a year after my husband died. I found an enormous need to connect with other widows and widowers, but didn't like going to bereavements groups or meeting strangers in person. A lot of books I read talked about the emotional mechanics of loss, but not the logistical stuff, like maintaining a house by yourself or taking off the wedding ring. I wanted other people's opinions on such topics, so I created a site whereby people could write down their ideas and send them to me—anonymously if they wished. I also wanted to show others that there is no one way to get through the after journey and they are not alone. By that time, I had learned that I was okay doing it my way and that books with theories didn't meet my needs. The response I got on the site was tremendous. And I eventually had to do something with all my correspondence, which brings me to this book.

What follows is a collection of stories from other people who have endured various emotional changes and experiences during their first year after losing someone they loved. Some testimonials are angry, some are sad, and some happen to be funny. They are all raw, true, and unedited. While I had initially intended this book to be a guide for getting through the first and second year, exploring how others dealt with basic daily living—waking up alone, cooking for one, and deciding what side of the bed to sleep on—I think this book does more to show you that you're not alone more than anything else which gives you the strength to go on. Others are struggling through similar experiences in their own way. There can be no "how-to" when it comes to grief and finding a way to survive during those unique, isolating moments. You'll move forward and make transitions in your own time frame. You don't have to read this book in order of the pages. You can flip to other parts and find passages that speak to you.

I hope this helps you feel understood and not so alone. I've changed names of individual people to preserve their privacy. This in not about who said what—it's about what people shared during their most painful, vulnerable moments.

Good Things Always,
Laurie-Ann Weis
May 2005
www.laurieannweis.com

Part 1

The Beginning

The Moment

*W*hy did you go? Why did you leave me behind to "finish my lessons," as you liked to call them? I can't do this by myself. I don't want to walk this earth alone, and endure all of life's experiences solo. No second opinion. I can't share everything with you anymore. All these emotions I have to experience on my own.

> *Worry.*
> *Sadness.*
> *Frustration.*
> *Stress.*
> *Guilt.*
> *Anger.*
> *Pain.*
> *Joy.*
> *Love.*
> *Happiness.*

If something makes me happy, sad, or mad, I can't look to you for a response or support. You're only a memory now, an image in my head. All I can do now is say, "You would have loved this..." or "You would have picked the blue one over the red one..." or "You would have told me to let the anger go and focus on something else..."

My world is reduced to a bunch of would-haves.

It's never planned. We wake up, get ready for the day, check our calendars to make sure everything is covered. Then BANG...one moment in time changes our lives forever.

It was a special day. Steve and I were on vacation. We were standing together in a museum talking about black pottery. I asked him a question and he didn't answer. I looked up at my handsome, healthy, hazel-eyed husband. His head was tilted to the left and he was drooling. After the paramedics arrived, we found out Steve had had a seizure. Three weeks later we found out he had fourth stage lung cancer and brain tumors. Steve had 18 months to live with treatments or three months without treatment. The terror and disbelief were indescribable. A survivor mode set in. I tried to stay in control. We made a plan. We followed it. We had to win. He was my everything. We lost. Steve died January 8, 1999. I walked into the den to find him sitting upright in his bed, his arms splayed out as if he were an angel. He wasn't breathing. He was gone. I fell to the floor on my knees and screamed like a wild animal.

The last eight months my husband was paralyzed, incontinent, and eventually lost all his eyesight. I was praying for the Lord to take him at the end. I felt like I lost him twice. First, after his brain surgery, which took a brilliant man and reduced him almost to a child, and then the ever so slow deterioration of his body functions, dictated by his brain. It was hellish. We had been married 13 years. I had two children from a previous marriage that became his. We were so close. I always told everyone that I had to go to the end of the earth to find him.

~Natalie C.

I lost my husband to a massive stroke four and a half years ago. It still feels like yesterday. I'll never get over it. "Closure?" Who ever coined that word? There is no such thing. I'll always have a hole in my heart.

~Ann G.

I lost my husband nine months ago in a motorbike accident. We have a two-year-old son. I feel that I am living in a dream world still waiting for him to walk through the door. I still have all his clothes in our closet. I haven't moved his possessions. I talk about him all of the time because it keeps him alive. It hasn't sunk in yet to our son that Daddy isn't coming home. I keep thinking in my mind that he is just working away from home and I still text his mobile phone, which was put in his coffin with him. I can never ever imagine being as happy again.

~Kimberly D.

My husband was killed in the capsizing of a 120-foot dive boat during a hurricane. I miss him so much that it causes physical pain. Learning from the investigators that this accident could have been prevented by the boat owners, makes it worse.

~Megan T.

We were so happy with each other and our lives. Our daughter was happily married. One day, we got a call from our daughter that while on their vacation, my son-in-law had a seizure, which resulted in brain and lung cancer. I broke into a sob and said, "It wasn't suppose to happen like this. I'm supposed to go first." My wife put her arms around me crying and said, "It's just not your turn." The real pure feeling of joy in our lives disappeared that day and never returned.

~Hyman S.

    My husband had bladder cancer. After years of brutal treatments with the hope to live a quality life, the cancer went into remission. It popped up a few months later in his lungs. We continued to try to live a quality life. We had been married 30 years. He chose no further treatments. At 86, he decided he had lived a full life and would help me to live alone. Even though I believed that I was prepared for his death and had counted my blessings, the shock of being alone is nothing that you can prepare for. I withdrew and turned off my emotions because the pain was more than my body could handle physically or emotionally. I may as well have died the same day he died.

~Jennifer L.

The Truth About Grief

I *can't do this without you. I miss you so much. Please come back to me. I know you tried to live. I know you did everything you could to survive your illness and get better. I know you did what you could to make sure I'd be okay once you were gone. I know you fought as hard as you could all the way to the end. But I just can't do this. It's impossible to prepare feelings for after death. It doesn't work. I can't go back to being single again like I was so many years ago. I'm not the same person. I don't know what it's like to be single anymore. I was so used to you as being half of me. We were one. Please come back!*

I received my masters in Human Behavior and Psychology. I knew the death process because I had studied it in books. Denial, grief, anger, and resolution. Oh yes, and then you move on. It's not that easy to do or simple to understand when you are drowning in it.

I learned from experience that there are two kinds of pain. There is physical pain and emotional pain. Physical pain was a knife stabbing inside my stomach ripping at my flesh. It was so painful that I lay in bed holding on to my side. *My heart felt carved out. I could visualize the gashes in my mind. Physical pain is something you feel soon after the death. One psychologist described this as the time when the heart and soul of your loved one is being removed from Earth. This physical pain extends from two strong souls torn apart, going in different directions. And when your soul repairs itself following this cut and separation, the physical pain ends. At that point, you have to keep fighting the emotional pain, which is what takes away your happiness, your joy, and your hope. It affects everything you do.*

When I was going through this, I couldn't remember what I read. I would walk into a room and forget why I went there. I would listen to a friend and not hear what she said. Emotional pain made me snap at people. It made me rude. I would cry at the drop of a hat. It took away my dreams, hopes, and sense of safety. It changed my relationships with friends and family. It made me someone I was not.

I was still here on Earth. I could feel Steve's spirit, but I had to do a different journey now. Alone. The release of my physical pain had to run on its own timeline. It took three months before that pain left. One day, I woke up and my body felt normal. I knew something was different when I opened my eyes. The stabbing and carving was gone from my heart and stomach. The feeling of normalcy was so foreign to me that at first I didn't trust it. When I pushed myself out of bed, I felt the weight of my body but not the bruises. The pain was still in there, but no longer tied to my bones and joints. It was latched to the ethereal parts—the spirit and the mind. The physical pain waned for a few days and came back sporadically like a bad rash. But then the pain-free periods lengthened and the time in between good and bad days became fewer and fewer. Eventually, the physical pain was gone.

I became stronger when I only had to deal with

the emotional pain. I took each morning, each afternoon, and each evening slowly. I moved forward in slow, itty-bitty increments. Sometimes it did feel like I was moving backwards or sideways, anything but forward. Everything was a memory. The happiest moments, like birthdays, holidays, and the discovery of good news were now the hardest times to get through because they dragged my mind back to memories. I knew I had a choice: let grief take over me and disappoint Steve's memory by failing to go on and be happy with the rest of my life, or I could honor myself and Steve's memory by choosing joy, working toward happiness, and accepting a future for myself.

Our wounded hearts get used to scabs. Time gives us the scabs so we can find a way to laugh, play, love, and feel that there's more purpose to life again. Occasionally those scabs get ripped off and we bleed all over again. I don't know if those scabs ever really go away for good. Someday, we can find joy again, differently, but we can't see that now.

I find grief to be an all-encompassing, intense and overwhelming emotion. In intensity, it is comparable only to love. It is as devastating as love is uplifting. It is the antithesis to love. It is my belief that the degree of grief is dependent upon the degree of love. In my life, those were the only two emotions that overtook my being. My actions were controlled by both. In love, I disobeyed my parents and fought for my guy; in grief, I defied nature and attempted suicide.

~Bobbi W.

Grief to me is getting in the car and crying all the way home, hearing a song that reminds me and tears my heart out. It's spending long weekends and holidays all alone. It's avoiding the places you went together, the reminders. Grief is such a shock that it may manifest itself by forgetting things, short time memory loss, and immune system deficiency. It's the feeling of emptiness and hopelessness. Grief is something you learn to live with. Grief is like doing time.

~Giselle V.

Grief to me is feeling numb to everything around me except my family, and well, so often I feel numb to them. It has been two and a half years for me now. I can't really believe it. The days blend into months and years. The world has moved around me and I know I have achieved so much in that time but I can't recall what I have done or why I did it. Did it happen yesterday or a month ago? I somehow drifted through yet another month of mere functioning. I look normal but my inner turmoil is eating at me like a leech. Each school term I vow to do reading every night with the boys and help with homework. Five months of this school year have passed. When I looked at the form where there should be over 100 little signatures to say my child has read to me, I saw only two. How ashamed I feel that I cannot get back to the person I once was. "Oh, you look great," they say. "Yeah, I feel fantastic!" Did I really just say that? Oh well, they believed me. It's okay. No, it's not. I don't recall names or places. Very little seems to come to mind of the 15 years I spent with my husband. It seems that when he died, so did my memory of our life. I don't cry for him. Nothing was left unsaid and he adored me and our babies. It was his time and we had half a lifetime. I just have to finish my other half here.

~Linda F.

Grief to me is: looking at your husband's picture, holding it close and crying; getting ready to wash his last soiled clothing and smelling his scent on the clothes and yearning for his presence; having something break, like the lawnmower, something he could have fixed in a heartbeat and feeling totally overwhelmed at the prospect of having to find a repair person to call.

~Gina G.

Grief to me is: the empty feeling after reaching over instinctively at night and no one is there; the deafening quiet of a house once filled with happy banter; the anger inside because after the funeral, everyone's lives continue on, uninterrupted, and yours lies in pieces like a broken glass; the panicky feeling that no one will worry if you don't make it home by six, or if you have an emergency, no one will miss you until you don't show up for work; the reminder that you no longer make the same significant difference in anyone else's world; the loneliness you feel day after day from no longer hearing the words, "Honey, I'm home," and the longing for the personal endearments such as "I love you."

~Jayne D.

I don't know if it is because we're having so much rain, but it surely is raining inside, too. I've told my friend that each person has 16 gallons of tears that they have to use up. I think I'm about up to 13 by now. I have finally admitted to my counselor that God has left me, too. I told her I thought it was my job to look for God. She didn't quite agree and she thought that I shouldn't try so hard. What about faith? Does it just go sometimes?

~Patricia H.

Anger

Your car worries me. The alarm goes off randomly especially in parking lots. I have no clue how to turn it off. I tried to find the paperwork on it, but I gave up and took it into the dealership to see what I could do. I worry about re-injuring my back while driving. I worry about pressing too hard on the brake pedal or jarring my spine out of whack again. I can't have a relapse now that you're gone. I know that you did your best teaching me how to handle the car. Right before you were bedridden, remember? I guess I just have to lessen my fears with practice. Everybody is patient. Everybody is loving and caring and all that. But no one is you. No one can be you or replace you.

My anger was huge and unwieldy. It appeared a year after Steve died. During the first year, I was so consumed with grief and sadness that I had no strength to be angry. But the anger came like a tidal wave and it knocked me down and kept pulling me out to sea even when I tried to get up. I was angry at life for being so unfair. I was angry that he suffered. I was here, alone. He promised me he would never leave me. I would always be safe. Well, he left!

At age 18, a car accident shifted the course of my life and taught me how to deal with anger and devastation because its resulting consequences meant living with a bad back and never bearing children. But the anger following Steve's death was different. It wasn't an anger I knew how to suppress or manage. I closed down, shut most everyone out. I didn't see the patterns of my anger until I mouthed off rudely at a business conference, and was so embarrassed by my own behavior that I quit the organization two days later. My mouth was out of control. I couldn't recognize my feelings of anger as they were building. If I could, I would have vented them elsewhere. It wasn't my intention to hurt anyone.

As time passed, I could feel the anger stewing inside like an erupting volcano. I learned that ignoring it wouldn't make it go away. I needed an empathetic ear. No one could solve this. I was overwhelmed by the intensity of my own emotions, and tried to find ways of easing the anger. I needed to let the anger subside and I needed to learn a new set of social skills. I began with golf, taking putting lessons and asking my instructor to drive me around the course to admire the flowers, the ponds, and the peace in the trees. It was about being on the golf course and not keeping score. I also decided it was time to take singing and dancing lessons. I hadn't danced in more than 30 years because of my back, and here I was, finally ready to do it all over again but with no one by my side.

I was lucky when it came to friends. I had a few friends who didn't judge me and who let me just cry and sound like a broken record. I avoided people who made my anger worse. I kept telling myself that I was glad that they didn't understand. I didn't want them to go through this pain. I got good with talking to myself and working through my pain. I did a lot of talking to the ceiling fan while I lay down at night. The walls of my bedroom were a comfort to me, and I had gotten used to staring at the fan whirling around and around like a musical beat to my musings before falling asleep. The ceiling fan had become a backboard for my own thoughts.

My husband always promised that life would go on easily because we had friends, family and hobbies. I tried to believe him. A month later, I realized life had drastically changed and what was constant and steady no longer existed. I was so emotionally lost and angry that he left me, even though I knew it wasn't his choice. He was sick and he died. I would stand in front of his picture and ashes and yell, "You lied to me. I hate you for it. Why did you lie to me? Life is so hard without you."

~Nicole C.

I lost my husband to a massive stroke four and a half years ago. It still feels like yesterday. I'll never get over it. Closure! Whoever coined that word? There is no such thing. I'll always have a hole in my heart but one learns to live with it.

~Paula J.

I am resentful that I have been robbed of my freedom. I am a mum and had little freedom before but my husband and I shared the babysitting because we didn't want our kids with babysitters. When he died, I was so angry, I went against what we believed and left the kids with sitters on a regular basis. I knew they hated it and I felt extremely guilty. I started to party. I was out of control and everyone knew it. I snapped. My husband died unexpectedly in February and I never grieved. I had been strong for everyone else. Now it was November and I just lost it. It's my turn to be looked after.

~Marilyn P.

My husband died when I was 35 years old from a massive heart attack. The anger I felt was tremendous. I was angry with myself for not administering C.P.R. properly. I was angry with God, the Why Me? syndrome but most of all I was angry at my husband! How mean of him leaving me alone! I asked the funeral chap if he would feel cold to touch and he said, "Yes." They left me alone with his body. I kissed him. Then I shouted with all my might, "How could you?"

~Maggie O.

I was so angry last night that my daughter refused to go to sleep. I banged my husband's picture real hard on my bedside table and shouted, "Why did you leave me so early?" I was driven up the wall and I just burst out crying.

~Germaine D.

Ashes

You're still in the front closet, behind the suitcases. Sometimes when I open the closet to retrieve batteries, my coat, or the suitcases, I know that I am near you. I know I said that I'd dump you into the ocean, but I haven't found a boat I'd like to go on, or the courage to get rid of what remains of you. I thought a time would come when it'd make sense to scatter your remains, but that time has not come. I can't bear to part with them. At first, your ashes gave me the creeps but as time went on, I'd walk down the hall and smile as I glanced at the closet door. It was my secret.

Steve and I decided that we both wanted to be cremated. Since my mother and stepfather lived fifteen minutes from the cemetery, they picked the ashes up and held on to them. My mother placed them on her rocking chair in the den for weeks. She spoke to them every day and cried when she eventually handed them over to me. His ashes were in a box inside a blue velvet bag.

"Can I have some of these ashes, Laurie?" she asked me with wet eyes.

"What? I can't believe you'd ask such a thing," I said

quickly, taking the box. I noted the pain in her eyes and the comfort that his ashes probably brought her. We never spoke about it again.

Six years later, the ashes still remain in the closet. I don't think about them very often but when I do, I smile. I'm not sure when or if I will follow through with my promise of tossing them out to sea. Now, I feel like Steve is just safe, with me, where no one can touch, probe, hurt or infect him. I will guard his earthly remains as he continues to shelter my soul.

When Steve died, a part of me died with him. Getting through the funeral was an act of God. I didn't feel anything for days and cried endlessly until I passed out from exhaustion. My eyes could barely see through the sea of tears. I didn't read, listen to the radio, watch television or keep up with anything going on in the world for months. I had to deal with God all over again, this time from the other side of broken—from the side where I was now alone and would have to ask the Whys, What Nows and Whens.

There were no rules and as long as I kept moving forward, it just didn't matter where the ashes were placed.

My husband wanted to be cremated and have his ashes disposed. I couldn't live with that because I needed him in one spot. We decided I would keep the ashes and my children would bury me in a casket with his ashes. His ashes now sit on the nightstand by his side of the bed with his picture, his glasses and his cologne.

~Cecilia A.

I finally made a decision after a year. I'm going to bring my husband's ashes home and keep them here with me for a while. I just haven't found a way to connect with him and thought maybe, if I had a little shrine, I'd feel connected again.

~Marlene K.

I had my husband's ashes in my bedroom for five weeks because he wanted his best friend and his brother to be with me when his ashes were scattered in Lock Lomand. I used to say, "Good night, Barry. Lots of love." When his ashes were scattered, I wanted to gather them back. One thing that still makes me smile is the memory of bringing Barry's ashes home, initially. The cab driver could smell the formaldehyde. When he asked me for the fare, I said, "Ask him. I would have walked!" He did look at me a bit strangely but at that point in grief, I didn't care what anyone thought.

~Margaret B.

There were no ashes. He was buried as a whole man. I could not bear the thought of cremation. To me, burning his body would have been destroying the man even further, killing him again, causing him more pain. That is weird, I know, as he is already dead. But Jesus was not cremated and I believe we should as believers follow His way.

~Mary L.

My husband was cremated. I chose the fuss-less way because land is scarce in Singapore and eventually the government would get you to exhume the body so I would prefer to do it now, rather than later and rekindle those past memories. It's too painful for me to deal with. Cremation is a more common method now in Singapore and we store our loved ones ashes in columbariums and my husband's ashes are in a Christian columbarium in the western part of Singapore. Thankfully, this is a very beautiful, elegant-looking place that is clean, bright, airy and peaceful. Its architecture won some awards as well and it's operated by a group of Christian churches in Singapore. I enjoy this place. Actually, the Chinese do not believe in storing the ashes at home for fear of breaking the urn. It's just how we feel and we could care less what others think.

~Lynn Q.

I was emotionally numb when I went to identify my husband's body. Then I saw him looking great. No signs of the illness. He looked rested and peaceful. His skin was so smooth. I bent over and kissed him and thought, "Gee, he feels cold." I felt like he was alive and I should put a blanket on him.

~Norma G.

Shrine

$\mathcal{I}$'ve started to take down your shrine. I hired the 14-year-old boy next door to help me. He packed everything up and put the box in the garage. I spent the rest of the weekend patching up the tiny nail holes. I had two large framed accomplishments of my own that had never been hung. I hung them in the middle of the wall that was mine now. It was time. It feels good. I have to move forward on my timeline, my way. There are no rules.

I have many pictures of you throughout the house but they are mixed with my new life and my past life. I remind myself that I have been lucky and that I am not alone. I will continue to add new pictures to my collection as my life continues to unfold.

When I met my husband, he had never been celebrated for his accomplishments. Awards, published articles about him, articles he wrote, covers of his published books, and personal pictures were placed in a large folder on the floor in the back of his closet. Six months later, I had an entire wall above his desk covered with framed articles, pictures, plaques, awards, and knickknacks celebrating his accomplishments.

My husband loved art and photography. We had family pictures from floor to ceiling on a wall unit in our den. After he died, the framed accomplishments on the wall were referred to by my friends as, "The Shrine." The first year, a few people told me to take it down because I couldn't move forward. The wall stayed. It gave me peace. The second year, I took down the majority of the den pictures on the wall unit and put up a lot of pictures from my past and present. My goal was to prove to myself that I had a life before Steve and that I would have a life after Steve. I needed convincing. However, Steve's personal wall of accomplishments remained and I worked at his computer sitting under it.

Things changed in year two. One day a male friend of mine stood before "The Shrine" and said, "There isn't a man on this Earth than can live up to Steve. You've got to take this down and move forward. You are still alive. You are single." The words stung. The tears dripped from both of our eyes.

I put up a collage of more than 50 pictures of my wife on the wall of my bedroom and hall. It gave me something to do and the pictures are beautiful memories. A few people commented that I had made a shrine of my wife who never really liked to have her picture framed. The pictures were taken down when I had to move. After I relocated, I put up one collage with my wife and all of our family and I put our wedding picture up with a cross above it. The pictures give me peace because they were of happy times. I think we start to bend as people give us advice to move forward with our lives. We can remove pictures but we can't remove our memories.

~Mark R.

It's been two months since my husband has passed on and I've finally taken down the sympathy cards.

~Nicole Y.

༄

I put his ashes, glasses, cologne, and favorite picture of him on the night stand by his side of the bed. It's been there for a year. I kneel in front of it and cry. It's cathartic.

~Anne D.

༄

My study is his shrine. Photographs of us are on the walls. I also have VHS tapes of us singing together. I first met my husband as a bass guitar player with curly hair. I fell head over heals for him!

~Patricia R.

༄

I could not create a shrine fast enough. I started out with two shrines. One altar was made with his mother's dresser and the other was a small table. I used his VA marker because I had purchased a double marker with both of our names inscribed. I could not imagine in my wildest dreams placing that beautiful marker with the words, Korean War Veteran, outside to be rained, snowed and trampled on by stupid people who had no respect for veterans, least of all the dead! I have had his flowers and flags stolen right off his grave! When my husband was alive, he always said, "The Korean Vets were forgotten." He was right. I now have one shrine with his marker and three beautiful angels. Two angels are white and one is gold. It is truly beautiful and it comforts me. It has been up for four years and it is staying up!

~Paula O.

I don't believe in shrines or altars at my place. In fact, after I redecorated, I removed my husband's picture (used at the wake/funeral) from the hallway table leading to my bedroom because my father-in-law was always coming and standing there to pray to my husband, which to me was an altar in the making. My religion forbids us to create idols and shrines as a form of worship. My husband is always in my heart and that's good enough.

~Tanya K.

I want the shrine, the pictures, the mementos…and yet, they only bring on tears and do not help me to move on.

~Sheila W.

Alone in Bed

$\mathcal{J}$ stared at our bed. Which side of the bed should I sleep on? My side is so lonely but I can't go on your side. I don't want to mess it up. Are you really gone? Maybe it's just a nightmare and I'll wake up. I crawled into the middle of the bed and I reached for your hand. We always held hands as we went to sleep. I can't find your hand. Your smell is gone from your pillow.

Days passed. I changed sides. Maybe if I moved to where you slept I could feel you. Your side of the bed is foreign to me. I feel raw. I feel like my heart is bleeding again but there is no blood on the sheets. My emotional pain is so huge. I want to cuddle with you. I want to lie on top of you with your arms around me. I miss feeling safe. I miss being held. So I reached for the stuffed kangaroo that sat on the chair. I held it and I wondered, "Will I ever be held again?"

My first Valentine's Day without my love was so empty that I sobbed until I fell asleep. While I was sleeping, magic happened. Steve came to me in a dream. In it, I was in our bathroom sitting on my makeup chair in front of my *table and smoothing cream on my face. Steve appeared in light blue 505 jeans and a short-sleeved Greenline shirt, which is like a golf shirt but blousier with a finished edge. He had a full head of brown hair and his skin glowed. His body was healthy and strong. I remember calmly looking up at him and saying, "I knew you would come back. You didn't leave me."*

"I'm not here," Steve said gently.
"Yes, you are," I corrected him.
"I'm okay and you're okay," he said.
"I'm okay?" I questioned.
"I'm okay and you're okay," my husband reassured me.

And then he disappeared. I woke up. I sat up in my bed confused and shaken. I looked around, taking in this real moment. I could feel Steve's presence and I could smell his Polo aftershave in my mind. When I came to my senses and acknowledged that this was a dream, I sunk myself back under my white down comforter and said aloud, "Thank-you for coming to me." I smiled for the first time in weeks and fell back to sleep. This was just one of the many exhalations I'd experience in this after journey.

I practically fall off the bed staying on my side. I don't want to mess his side up. I know he's not there but it makes me feel less lonely if I don't reach over and find him missing.

~Jessica S.

For the first year, I found myself gravitating over to his side of the bed. I wanted to sleep where he slept. It is the beginning of my second year without my husband and I have started to go back to "my side." I find it isn't nearly as comfortable for some reason. Sleeping alone in this house was my first big mountain to climb. Except for his hospital stays, I couldn't remember the last time I had slept alone.

~Shirley D.

The "bed" my husband and I shared was at the beginning of our relationship as husband and wife. It was the first major purchase we made for our condominium. When I first met my husband, he was the consummate bachelor. He had proudly purchased his first home, a condominium. It was beautifully furnished. He had superb taste, refined and very sophisticated for a "guy." However, the bedroom was a bare room and contained nothing but a three-dimensional sculpture on one wall and track lighting. The first priority after we married was to purchase a bed because it was a bit uncomfortable for two grown people to sleep on a sofa! We had a great time looking for a comfortable bed and so pleased when it arrived. Each night we would curl up together, holding one another close and waking up beside one another to start each day...not to mention enjoying lovemaking.

My husband's illness meant I moved out of our bedroom. Instead, an oxygen concentrator, a bedside commode, and a variety of medical equipment moved in. My husband had many nights of restlessness with pain, and difficulty breathing. During the last few months, his body was wracked with such horrible pain that the slightest movement was torturous. Often, I would help him into bed and he would look at me and plead for me to lie next to him. He would say, "Please hold me." I would lie next to him and put his head on my shoulder until he went to sleep. As time went on, my husband could no longer get onto our big king size bed and I had to have a hospital bed delivered. The day the hospital bed arrived, my husband was adamant about not sleeping in it. I tried to hold back my tears as I explained that the bed would allow us to elevate his head to make breathing easier and that he could get into bed without the pain of lifting his legs so high because this bed could be lowered. Yet, each night he would go to "our" bed and stand beside it waiting for me to help him. He never slept in that hospital bed. I could not bear to see him standing next to our bed without giving in so I would prop up the pillows and call our son to help put dad to bed…in our bed.

After his death, and the entire following year, I could not sleep in that bed. I would go into the room and see him there waiting for me. The darkness would bring the sadness in a rush around me. I slept on the sofa that entire year, closing off the bedroom that we shared. I tried rearranging the room but it did not help. Finally, I moved out of the condo and put our bed into my new bedroom. The first night I slept on our bed. I felt his presence and a sense of peace. The sadness was gone. I felt him lying next to me in spirit and I was comforted. Now another year later, I am shopping alone for a new frame, headboard, and footboard but will keep our box spring and mattress. Now I hold the memories of that first shopping expedition with love and I remember how happy we were then. I remember how my handsome husband and I were trying out the mattresses in the store, giggling like two overgrown children. I remember him saying in the throes of illness, "Hold me," and I ask him to "Hold me" now as I move forward without him. He does, every night and each sunrise; his memories keep me close to him.

~Nancy R.

After my husband died in our bed, my sister stayed in the room with me. When I woke up early in the morning and reached out to touch what I thought was my husband's hair, I noticed that it looked different and messy and I reached out to fix it. Of course my sister woke up and wondered what I was doing. I still stay on my side of the bed, hoping that Larry will somehow join me at night. After eighteen years together, I still think he is coming home. The saddest part is that I held him when he died. My head knows this, but my heart refuses to accept the information. The relationship we shared was that once-in-a-lifetime love, and I don't want to let go.

~Sylvia D.

It is so hard to sleep without my husband. I used to take one of his sweaters to bed just so I could smell him.

~Theresa H.

I couldn't reconcile the fact that my husband wasn't going to sleep by me anymore. I always relished the times I used to have him by my side and how nice it was as a couple to share the same bed. For now, my grandma-in-law sleeps with me on my husband's side so when we both retire to bed, it seems strange to have her by my side. I don't know if this is a good idea or not. It's just easier because she helps with my daughter if she cries at night. I had bad insomnia last night until the wee hours. You know how old ladies rarely sleep and love puttering around the house? When I hear her, I always imagine it's my husband. It's a very depressing feeling.

~Michelle C.

After eight months, I still can't sleep in our bed. I took to sleeping in the recliner in our family room, the place where he slept during the last weeks of his life because he couldn't sleep lying down. We used to sit there and watch TV together. Now I sleep there. I'm not sure if I sleep there because that's the last place he was in our house or because I just miss him in our bed. I don't think I can sleep in our room the way it was—I'm thinking about remodeling it to make it different. I feel I need to change some things. I really haven't decided what to do yet.

~Rochelle L.

I sleep on my "own" side of the bed as I've done for nearly 40 years but this just leaves a big empty space where my husband should be. Maybe I will eventually get a single bed, but will that feel as though I'm losing him even more?

~Nina J.

No More Hugs

At this moment, I feel so alone, so empty. I need a hug from you right now. I know you would hug me if you could. You tried to prepare me and you told me to find sunlight dancing on water. That would be you.

I run to the ocean. I can feel the heat of the sun on my shoulder. I know that's your energy but I can't feel your arms around me. I need to feel safe.

Everyone needs the human touch. A friend suggested that I get a massage. I never had a professional massage before. She said the human touch would be healing. It didn't help. I cried through the entire experience.

Your belief system gave my life focus, direction, and meaning. You were so good to me that I found myself speechless much of the time. You said you were words, while I was music. You never lectured or judged. We kept clear about our individual needs and never hesitated to share what we wanted. There was never an absolute right or wrong. We didn't compete with each other. We listened, cradled, encouraged, advised, loved, and inspired. We knew each other's boundaries and vulnerabilities.

Someone else suggested that I get a dog. That doesn't work for me.

I need to hold you and to feel your strength. I need

to cuddle with you. I bought a stuffed animal puppy and I have a stuffed animal kangaroo. I cuddle with them when I'm lonely and need to be held. I hug them when the silence in the house is deafening.

To Steve, the glass was always half full, and his job was to do the best he could with what life taught him. I, on the other hand, had trouble making peace with a lot of life's lessons. I sought sense in everything, including the nonsensicals. I thought, if I completed the lesson well and learned from it, then I wouldn't have that lesson again. I didn't want repeats and reruns in life, except in movies and songs. I craved time-outs between the lessons. It always seemed that after one lesson was learned, a new opportunity arose for another lesson immediately. I wanted a vacation from myself. But life doesn't work that way.

It was for this very reason that Steve was so important to me. He made life beautiful. He made everything seem endurable and meaningful.

By the time my husband succumbed to cancer, my decades-long struggles with my back were waning. I was stronger than I had ever been, and I was stuck with trying to understand why God would take away my husband just when I was healing. It wasn't fair. Steve would say his purpose on earth was to heal me so I could help children learn and grow into thoughtful, productive adults. Maybe in the grand scheme of things, that's true. But it's still wasn't fair.

I entertained many conversations with friends about life's hard lessons once Steve had died. I found peace in those discussions but not resolution. I didn't know myself because I was still stuck in Steve's love. I was detached from myself, hollowed out by his death. Nothing could fill the hole, not *even my best friends or faith in Steve's afterlife. I couldn't endure the thought of learning to live here on earth without him present. I was stuck in Stage One of the grief process: Denial.*

Problem was, I had to allow myself the rest of my life, which was something I wasn't ready to do. I remained detached for a long time—over a year, having no interest in attaching myself to the world again and regaining a sense of place and joy among the living. That would come later. I had to get through the after journey.

I am a recent widow…not quite three weeks. I miss the physical touch of my husband who was a touchy-feely person. He was not very good at verbalizing his emotions but I knew by his touch (holding hands as we fell asleep, kissing the back of my neck as I stood at the sink doing dishes). I am feeling so lonely even though I have good support from my children.

~Terre S.

I realize that I will get no more hugs from the person who loved me the most. He used to hug me every day. Sometimes, I close my eyes and try to relive the feel of his hugs. Sometimes I hope that he's there somehow hugging me.

~Erica P.

Having no one to hold me makes me envious of others when I see their other half hold them. I begin to reflect on the times my husband did that and how I took those gestures for granted. It's human. I've learned what I treasured after it was taken away from me. I long to have someone do that again for me, although I recognize it'll be later because I still have my husband in my heart.

~Sherry L.

My wife passed away six months ago. How do you make it through the day much less through the night? We were married for 41 wonderful years. It's hard to accept that I won't hold or hug her anymore. It's like half of me has been taken away. I feel so empty.

~Sam G.

Missing her hugs are just one of the many things that will bring a flood of emotions and tears to my eyes. As my wife went through many hours of chemo and radiation, she would lay her head on my shoulder and sleep. Even though she hurt and was scared, she felt safe there. On the night that she died in the hospital, when her breathing became very, very labored, I held her in my arms. When I could control my emotions enough to speak, I told her that I would always love her. During the final ordeal that she faced, which seemed to last an eternity, I tried as best as I could to comfort her between the outbreaks of asking God to please take her quickly so that she would not have to go through the agony of suffocating to death. There were times during her 90 days in the hospital when I would lose it and lay on her as she lay in bed. She would just rub my back and head and say, "I love you." Oh, for just one more hug and to hear her say, "I love you."

~Eric G.

I long so much for the intimacy we both shared. I think about it day in and day out. I am mindful that I don't get too obsessed about this. Sometimes at night, I brush this awful feeling aside but deep within, it's so painful. I am learning to hug my daughter more these days but the feeling is very, very different.

~Jamie Z.

Mail

You've been gone a few months. The mail keeps coming with your name on it. The hospital where you died sends you mail. Don't they know that you are dead? Some mail is addressed to Mr. and Mrs. or just Mrs. Steven S. Weis. It's always a reminder that you are gone and we are no longer a part of a couple. I am no longer a Mrs. I'm too old to be a Miss. Ms. surely doesn't feel right. I hate going to the mailbox. The sadness and anger at what was and is no more are fierce. I made a plan. I ordered 17 magazines...Town and Country, People, Allure, Orange Coast. Now when the mail comes, there is something nice and friendly at the bottom of the pile.

Later, the magazines expired. I reordered a few of them because I actually enjoyed them. I still recoil when I see my husband's name but I don't cry anymore. I say to myself with a smile, "My husband was incredible and will never be forgotten."

It's amazing how years have passed and those newsletters and junk mail and miscellaneous correspondence still arrive with his name printed boldly in the envelope window, as if he were standing behind a secret door. I've ripped off the return address and sent them back with a note saying he was dead. Well, in the beginning, I was polite and wrote, "Steve died on January 8th, 1999. Please remove his name from your list." As time went on, I went through an angry phase where I'd furiously write a note that said, "Steve is dead. Remove his name!" The hospital where he died sent him letters asking for a donation for two years after he passed away. Credit card companies continued to send pre-approved forms. The anger that followed the grief eventually turned into a bitter annoyance. Eventually, the anger and annoyance subsided.

Surprise! I thought I had changed names on everything. Every week, new envelopes arrive with his name. It's a stab in my heart. Now I just get angry. The worst is when people call up and ask to speak to him.

~Fran J.

Somehow, I was able to accept his name on the envelopes. I think it's because I'm a very neat and organized person. I wanted to clear whatever mail I had in the postbox and deal with it right away. The mail for my late husband was more of the legal matters. I was so concerned with settling the issues that I didn't look at his name, which helped to take my pain away.

~Sharlene B.

Initially, the first month, I was still feeling very numb from his death and robotic in my actions. I was checking the mail to get things done. But subsequently, the stabbing pain of realizing he was indeed gone and not able to pick up his own mail hit me. It reminded me that I have to do this all on my own. My husband used to check the mail and clear it every night. There are some letters that come for him and I feel compelled to call the organization to delete him from their mailing list but I find it too painful to break the news that he has passed on. Of course, I could say that he doesn't want to be on the list, but it's really against my principles to tell a white lie. So for now, I just throw out his mail.

~Anita B.

At first when I received mail with my husband's name on the envelopes, it reassured me that he couldn't be dead if people were still writing to him. Later, as the mail kept coming, I actually enjoyed contacting mail senders and saying, "Sorry, you won't receive a reply from my husband because he is dead!" I enjoyed their discomfort. That's not like me at all now but it was me then. Perhaps I was crazy at the time but it was a coping mechanism.

~Tania S.

It infuriated me to receive mail with my husband's name on it. I would get credit card applications with his name. I would cure myself and say things like, "My God in heaven. He is dead, dead, dead! Are you so desperate for customers that you give credit to the dead?" I would write to them and call them just to give them a piece of my mind. It didn't help. I even got more letters in the mail with his name on it. There is no justice for widows and widowers.

~Amanda E.

Credit card applications still arrive saying "pre-approved." You would think these people would do a little research before sending out this stuff.

~Carole H.

I don't know why this hurts so, but I still get mail for my husband and he has been gone now for two years. Some people say this can go on for years and it's beginning to make me angry. I've even called several places to have his named removed from credit card mailing lists, etc. It's a physical pain to turn over that envelope and see his name. Why can't they get it? Why can't they understand how important this is? Obviously, they have never lost anyone important to them or they would know.

~Cathy M.

Shopping for One

*H*olding hands and strolling through stores was a pure delight when we were married. How I loved watching you pick out things for me. I felt like a princess in fairyland. You were not the striking type easily plucked from a crowd, but boy did you look handsome in a tailored suit! I loved how you looked so regal in your suits. Picking out your clothes gave me a rush. I was magically drawn to you; the brilliance in your eyes was what captured me every time I looked at you—right down to the last moment. Oh, how I wish I could steal you away from Heaven for an afternoon of strolling, shopping, driving with the sunset. I miss those long afternoons.

It took me a long time to go back to the men's departments once he was gone. The beautiful clothes, and the smell of the colognes could sink my heart. It was uncontrollable. I felt a deep emptiness that reminded me that my love was gone, taking me to an unbearable place of loneliness.

I learned to organize my errands close to home in little strip malls so driving was minimized. No longer a passenger in a car with a man who'd drive up the coast *singing, eating energy bars and making errands fun, I was now in the driver's seat doing life for myself. I needed new systems for living. The old and familiar ones wouldn't work in my new solo life. Costco's carts were too large and the food quantities too big for me to handle on my own. Favorite stores were too far away for me. It had been a long time since I'd shopped on my own and made decisions on my own, even the trivial ones like picking out new items for the house, deciding on a movie to rent, or an assortment of fruits and vegetables from the local market.*

I felt lost, unable to define who I was now. I was aloof in grief and no one could bring me back to any sort of reality. Not even I could do this. I felt like a baby. There was so much to manage beyond the grief. I had to re-learn basic things in everyday life, and combine it with how grief made me feel. Vulnerable. Weak. Depressed to the point where you can't imagine brushing your teeth alone. I was forty-seven years old and had been so sheltered up to now because of my back problems, that being independent was terrifying.

It's so difficult to walk through a men's department in a clothing store. My husband wore clothes beautifully and I enjoyed shopping for him. I see things and I think, "He would look great in that." I get a stomachache and walk out.

~Sally S.

Seeing men's things in stores is very difficult. Last night, a catalogue with men and women's clothing came in the mail. It hurts so much to see men's clothing that I can't look at the pages. I always enjoyed buying a lot of my husband's clothes, especially items he would never purchase for himself. He enjoyed what I brought home because he liked looking good and he trusted my taste. I received as much pleasure buying the clothes as he did receiving them. I now try to avoid the men's department unless I absolutely have to buy a gift for someone.

~Kathy R.

⁀

We always did the shopping together, and it was such a joy. Now, I don't care anymore and just buy the necessities.

~Kristin J.

⁀

This might be a blessing in disguise because I never shopped for my husband. He was a very tall person with long limbs so he had to try on the clothes before they were purchased. But when we did shop together, we bought so many things and truly enjoyed it.

~Laura S.

⁀

The initial month of his death, I went shopping with a friend who came to visit me from Malaysia. I envy seeing couples shop together and the lady holding a shirt on her partner's back to see if it would fit. It reminded me of what I used to do. The pain came back and I stared at them for a split second before resuming shopping. Deep within, there is a sense of emptiness. I yearn for my husband to be back so that we can shop together.

~Joan T.

I still avoid the men's department and it has been a year. I hate that I have no one to buy for. My husband was not a shopper. Sometimes, while I am in a store, I get the feeling of panic and have to leave. Especially grocery shopping. All of his favorite foods jump off the shelves at me. I shopped "for him."

~Janis C.

I seem to be able to find someone else to shop for besides myself. I'm a "just because" little gift buyer. I have a daughter, a son, their spouses, and four grandchildren. When I see something I think any one of them might like, I buy it. Of course my husband used to be on the list, too, but he was never the only one. With food it's more difficult. The grocery store presents moments of sadness.

~Beth R.

I find it pathetic trying to decide what to buy when I really don't care about eating. Just seeing some of the items in the supermarket makes me feel very sad. There were some things that I always made sure that he had, things he especially liked even thought I didn't. Just seeing those things can almost bring me to my knees. I hate going to the market and I am usually so depressed by the time that I leave, I'm a mess. Then there is the issue of putting things away. The refrigerator, cabinets and pantry seem so empty. Lately, just getting through each day has been harder than before. I think I've actually realized that this is final and real. I just don't like it at all.

~Tess W.

Cooking for One/ Eating Alone

You *ou did all of the cooking. I set a beautiful table and washed the dishes. We never watched television while we ate. We only wanted each other's company. Every evening meal was like dining out. Now, I microwave the bare minimum. I stand at the kitchen sink and eat. Sometimes I sit at the table and watch the television or read the paper. I'm not sure what I read and I certainly can't tell you about what I am watching. It's really just noise. The food has no flavor. I need to eat to live. Do I want to live? I guess I do because I keep swallowing the food.*

The shock of my husband's death was soon followed by the shock of being alone. I didn't have young children to tend to or be whisked away by, into a larger world of shared grief. My lump of grief was my own and it was heavy. So many things I'd have to do by myself and for myself. Cook. Eat. Plan. Drive. Shop. Socialize. Vacation. Pay bills. Write checks. Maintain the books. Get through the holidays. Be happy alone. Find company within myself.

It sounds pathetic to say one cannot do these things alone when so many do. But once you've grown accustomed to sharing the duties and responsibilities of life with a soulmate, it's hard to go back to being alone and doing things solo. It's like you've suffered a stroke and you have to re-teach your legs to walk, your hands to reach out to objects and take hold of them, and your mouth to smile by inching it upward. Everything now was "for one." Table for one. Grocery shopping for one. Cooking for one. Bedroom for one. Holiday decorating for one person's enjoyment.

To think I'd have to rely upon myself for even the simplest things, like squeezing ice out of their molds in the freezer for my back when it hurt so much I could barely move, reaching for something high in the closet, or even taking the trash out when it rained, was troubling. Life had been perfect for a while and I hadn't imagined it being different until the cancer came and Steve went. Logic told me I'd never get him—or any person like him—back again. I didn't like people telling me "he's still with you" in some cosmic, spiritual way. If he was not on Earth to hold me, touch me, kiss me tenderly and tell me to my face that everything's going to be all right, then he was not really with me. I needed the real thing, the arms around me, the whispers in my ear, the long soft kisses and so on and so on. It was so hard to begin to make decisions for myself. I was on my own.

"Table for one, please…"

We never sat at the table when my husband was alive. We always sat in front of the TV. However, shopping is so different. When my husband was alive, he always came shopping with me and we always needed to buy a lot of vegetables, milk, bananas and cereal. It really added up!!

Food was really important to my husband. Now that I am on my own, I can buy whatever I want because I find it's a lot cheaper. Yet, I still can't get used to buying things like sushi and actually being able to make it into a meal! I make myself sit down and eat, even if it is in front of TV but I miss my husband's company.

~Mary Elizabeth S.

I find that at times, I'm still standing at the sink eating. It's hard to sit at the table. I watch television when I eat. We never ate with the television on. Shopping for one is brutal. I don't know what to buy.

~Beverly S.

It is hard to cook for myself. When my husband was alive, it was necessary to cook well-balanced meals and look after him. Now that I am on my own, it is harder to go through the effort of cooking even though I know it is important to cook well-balanced meals for myself.

~Tina T.

My first thoughts of eating alone in a restaurant were traumatic so I chose to go to a restaurant where the staff and owners had known us for years thinking that this would make it easier. One by one they greeted me. I sat down and it was so difficult. The realization of being alone was devastating.

~Sandy G.

When my husband was alive, I enjoyed experimenting with recipes because he enjoyed what I made. Now, I eat out of cans and I throw a piece of chicken or fish in a pan. I don't cook at all. Food doesn't interest me.

~Laurie J.

෴

I am so pathetic. I buy one squash, one potato, one yam. I unload it on the register counter and it's embarrassing. My food yells, "I AM ALL ALONE."

~Andi Q.

෴

Food shopping seems so pathetic to me. I try as hard as possible to avoid it. I keep seeing the things he liked and I can't get rid of the idea that I need to buy them. It just seems that everything is so very painful. I am always the one at the checkout with the frozen dinners, popcorn and ice cream. It even looks pathetic. It's so obvious that it's just for me. I just hate this whole thing and I just want my husband back.

~Joni G.

෴

I hate shopping for one. I can't think of what to cook for myself. I always cooked to please my husband. Therefore, I don't cook. I eat out a lot. I buy one of everything. One potato, one banana. I share my loaf of bread with the birds.

~Rita L.

෴

After eight months, it's still somewhat difficult to go to the supermarket. We usually went together because we both hated going and so we figured we'd suffer together. Right after his death, it was very, very difficult. Until I was standing in the market, I hadn't really thought about how going to the market would affect me. As I walked down the aisles getting what I needed, I saw items that only he would use. When I saw his particular favorite foods and drinks, I knew that I had to immediately leave the store because I knew I was going to break down and cry. I just got into my car and cried and cried. Now, when I go to the store, sometimes I'm okay, sometimes I'm not. I never know when something will trigger my sadness. It just happens.

~Ruth A.

Changing Phone Machine Message

The message on the phone machine says, "We are not home right now." If I erase it, does that scream out that you are gone?" Does, "I can't come to the phone right now" tell the whole world that I live here, alone, when they are living with their families?

At your office, although you were not sitting behind your desk, they kept your voice on your message machine for two months. I would call just to hear your voice say, "Have a nice day." Finally, I taped your message from a speakerphone. When your message was finally erased, I still had your voice wishing me a nice day. Your voice brought me comfort and set the tone for strength to get through another day. Oh, how I miss the sweet hellos and good-byes.

The strength of Steve's part of "we" grew weaker and weaker as the cancer battled onward and withered away at his very existence. I soon became the stronger part of "we" and seemed to be living independently for myself, but having to take care of my husband mightily in his last days. The

answering machine may as well have contained my voice alone. All the drugs, the brain radiation, and the cancer defeated my husband, relegating him to a bed in the living room until his passing. Despite my mantra to God to "take him or heal him but please don't let him suffer," from what I could tell, he suffered a little in his final days.

He was stuck in pain, or pain was stuck in him. Either way, he lost his independence in a short time. All that a man needs to feel independent, and in turn, dignified, dwindled. And he knew it. Shaving, flossing, cleaning, eating, and going to the bathroom. I took charge, holding the reins to his horse that was walking toward a grave. On my first day home alone, the phone would ring and ring and ring, and I'd be standing in the closet smelling his clothes. I didn't want to talk to anyone. Changing the outgoing message was not on my mind. Going through the messages that inundated my machine over the next few weeks wasn't on my priority list, either. I didn't change the outgoing message until six months later. How could I?

A friend called and my answering machine picked up. My husband's voice answered, "We are not available. Leave your name and number and we'll get back to you." She left a message saying, "Change that message. I can't stand it." When I returned her call, I said, "When I'm ready, I'll change it."

~Karen G.

I had no plan to change the message on my answering machine but fate did it for me. I couldn't take his voice off. I had friends ask me when I was going to do it. One day without thinking and without my glasses on I tried to erase some messages and I accidentally erased his message. I got hysterical, and cried as if he had just passed away. I called the answer machine company and found out it was permanently erased. I mourned for days over the loss of his voice.

~Carolyn S.

At first I was angry when someone called and asked for my husband. Didn't everyone know that my husband had died? Didn't the whole world know that he had died? And yet, I know that a loved one dies every day, not just my loved one but someone's loved one dies every day. I have learned to respond to them saying, "My husband died last October. Do you still wish to leave a message?" Sometimes they respond with a quick, "I'm sorry to hear that." Yet, they are off the line very quickly. I feel quite proud that I have not shed a tear during this encounter. I'm strong. Enduring is the rush.

~Kristine G.

It has been 10 months since my husband died. I now find that I can call back the person who phoned and say to them, "My husband died 10 months ago. Would you please remove his name from your calling list?"

~Lola W.

I miss my husband's voice a great deal. Even over a year later, I imagine him talking to me, his voice. I watch my wedding videotapes over and over just to hear his voice. It was very therapeutic for me because I felt comforted listening to his voice. I am so glad that I spent a small fortune making the video for our wedding. It serves its purpose today. On our wedding day, my husband dedicated a message to me, promising to take care of me until the end of time. He fulfilled it, but only for such a short period of our lives.

~Evelyn G.

Because of my children, I kept the machine "we" and nothing changed. I didn't change the outgoing message because my voice sounded so happy back then.

~Eva S.

I hear her voice a lot in my head. Well, it's not hers. But she was English and every time I hear and English accent, I look no matter where I am. It's been almost six years.

~David R.

Music/Television/ Pictures

The music stopped for me the evening after your funeral. I played our five favorite songs during the ceremony honoring you and then I shut off the music in our home. If you were words and I was music, well, the music died when you died.

I continued to watch all of our favorite television shows. The characters were like our old friends coming to visit me and I looked forward to their scheduled time. I left the pictures up on the wall unit in the den. It looks like a shrine to you now that you are gone. When you were here, it was just our life. Now I suppose it's my life.

I eventually played music again but nothing from our past. I listened to anything without memories, including pop music that would not have interested me earlier. I found a CD with songs written by a widow and sang her songs for a good cry. Those songs were my private release. One by one, the television shows went off the air. Old friends left. Old routines disappeared each season. A piece of me died each time, but I had to find replacements. Slowly, his shrine

came down and new pictures went up that didn't hint to his passing. I tried to convince myself that I had a life before him and that I would have a life after his death. It started to work. About two years into my after journey, I began to feel different. I began to feel a new kind of joy. By then, the music, television and pictures that we had shared were cycled out for new kinds of music, television shows and pictures. I still listen to oldies on the radio once in a while because they are "him" and not "us." "Us" music and "us" artists are just too painful. I'm not interested and I have worked hard to move on. I have new favorites now, music and artists my late husband never heard. I still find that I cling to songs about losing someone to death and I cry easily. It's almost like I need it to keep my soul cleansed of stagnant grief that slowly builds in my subconscious. Truth is, I learned that you never completely get over the loss of a loved one. The person is always in your heart and the scab rips off when you least expect it. Songs do that to me. But once cleansed, the scab grows back so I change the music and listen to songs about moving forward and loving again. My goal is to grow a thicker scab back quickly.

I can't listen to Frank Sinatra or any music that has memories. Music that he didn't care for brings me peace.

~Lorena P.

One of the hard moments for me was the first apple blossom of the year. "I'll be with you in apple blossom time," and he wasn't. Music was such a part of our lives, we both loved every type of music—pop, western and even classical. He sang a lot in the car, when alone or with someone.

Sometimes I'd get angry and upset when I got out of the car in the morning to go to work because I'd have some really dumb tune stuck in my head all day. Now when I hear those songs, it is really hard not to think how happy and content he was. Now I'm sad that I didn't take the time with him every day to enjoy his wry humor and dumb songs. Those songs, even just thinking about them, makes me cry—lots.

~Suzanna B.

I could not bear to watch TV shows that we had both loved. Nor could I watch movies or go to the movies anymore. The love scenes really get to me so I avoided them. Solution? No movies for that first year. Still, I remember the last movie, "As Good As It Gets," that we saw together. How ironic that this would be the title of the movie. It's sort of funny in a sick way.

~Irena C.

Forget about those love songs and oldies, the songs that we both loved. Our music followed me around everywhere, even into the supermarket and restaurants. I found a different type of music called light rock. I could not bear to hear "White Christmas" and it followed me everywhere. Every time I saw the snow, I thought about the song. I would love to bury that song in the snow! It took me three years to finally be able to listen to it and enjoy it again. I can listen to the other love songs now but at times, I still cry.

~Jo T.

I can listen to all music except love songs. I tried to listen to the last jazz CD that he bought, Nora Jones, one day before he passed on. I had no feelings really. I attempted to listen to the music we played at our wedding and it brought back many beautiful memories. Sometimes, I yearn so much for his presence to savor the music with me. I listen to our music occasionally but now it's dominated by my Christian prayer and praise music and my daughter's sing-a-long music.

~Patty L.

Pictures are everywhere in every room. I enjoy knowing he's here. I enjoy seeing pictures when he was young. I love seeing pictures of our happy times. Sometimes it brings tears to my eyes but it warms my heart.

~Leslie W.

Every time I look at my wedding and traveling pictures I scrutinize every inch of my husband. I look at the way he held me, the way we posed together and it brings tears to my eyes.

~Chawn M.

This is very hard. When I first met my wife in 1959, people didn't take photos like we do today. Luckily, I took a few pictures and I carry one of my favorites in my wallet. I never carried a picture of anyone in my wallet, not even my grandchildren. Now I carry three pictures of my wife in my wallet. I put a copy of one taken in 1959 on our grave marker.

My family said, "No, you're not dead yet." We laughed but my son and daughter said if that's what I want then to go ahead.

The first few months I couldn't sleep so I would get out all of the family albums and take my wife's pictures out one by one and put them in a new album that I made just of her. I have over 500 pictures in it now and she is in every one. It's funny how I remember where every one of them was taken.

A lot of the pictures were taken in England when we visited her family. They either let me take the pictures and make copies of them or they gave them to me to keep.

My wife was very pretty and modern. People would say how pretty she was and they just didn't say it to be kind. She turned heads and if you saw the pictures, you would know why.

I have promised one of my granddaughters that she can have the pictures when I'm gone. I know she will take care of them and pass them on. Sometimes when I'm alone, I look at them over and over. I never get tired remembering when and why they were taken and wishing I had taken one of her every day. My pictures of my wife are my treasures.

~Bill S.

I still don't listen to old love songs, watch sitcoms or watch old movies my hubby and I shared together. I just can't do it! Too painful!

~Gail F.

Love Letters/Notes

*D*o you remember the loves notes we'd pass back and forth?
I enjoyed the ones that had nothing to do with a holiday or
birthday. You were always so good with words. All of your
love notes filled me with enough love to last a lifetime. Or so
I thought. I miss those notes.

I did my best to return the favor, but I was never that
good with words. The best one I wrote was the one that I
gave to you about a month before you died. You were about
to go in for another round of radiation on your lung. But
things weren't working out with the treatments, and you were
fast approaching the end of your life. Nothing was working,
and I think I already knew that I was soon to be alone.
You had asked me about "purpose" the day before, and I
didn't know what to say. I didn't know what the purpose
of your cancer was and why your life had to be shortened.
Thoughts of purpose tore my sleep into pieces that night, and
I eventually slid out of bed to go write the longest Thank-You
letter I had ever written—and it was going to you. It was the
most important Thank-You letter I would ever write. Parts of
it went something like this:

"I'm writing this letter to you, not because you
don't know how I feel but because I love you so much and
appreciate everything about you. I am so overwhelmed with

gratitude for the time we have shared together. I am honored to be your wife, your friend, your lover, and your confidant.

"When I was a little girl, I dreamt about you. I wanted to marry my prince, a kind, gentle, understanding, non-judgmental, smart, loyal, loving, compassionate, generous, interesting man who had quiet power. A man who would be my soulmate, who loved me, and helped me to be my best self. A man I could share everything with—feelings, friends, business, and hobbies. And then you appeared out of nowhere. What a surprise! It was that energy.

"We always said it was like a shoe that fit. We became words and music. You came into my life when I could only stand on my feet for twenty minutes. I couldn't go out easily so you brought the world to me or moved mountains to take me places. You never once complained that I was an inconvenience. You were never embarrassed. You always said sharing an hour with me was better than going anywhere alone because we could laugh and sing and share our thoughts and feelings. When things were really rough for me, you said we'd eat cookies in bed and watch movies. Nothing was a problem for you.

Finding our first home together was special. You said, 'I think I found the perfect house for you. You'll be able to heal there.' And it was.

"The years moved on, we moved a few times for your job, but some things never changed. You always celebrated the 12th of every month because we met on the 12th. You were always there to share everything with me. If I needed something fixed, you fixed it or hired someone. If I needed to learn something, you taught me with patience and gentleness, even if I needed it repeated twenty times. You shared your business with me, telling me about your clients, partners, co-workers...and you embraced my working world. You cared about my world as if you knew each person. You embraced

my whole being. And get this: After almost thirteen years, you still hold my hand in the car as we drive, whether it's five minutes or two hours.

"I still can't believe any of this is happening. So many people around us are using alternative medicines and they are getting well. None of it makes sense to me. I don't understand the plan. I only know that you've touched many people in such a wonderful way. That is God's work. I just keep wondering, does God need you more than he thinks I need you? I hope not. You're all I ever wanted.

"Thank you for making me so safe with your words, actions and kisses. Thank you for giving my life passion and lust. Thank you for being. I will treasure you always. I see you in every beautiful garden. I see you in every beautiful sunset."

I love you, Laurie-Ann.

I was a lucky lady. My husband sent me flowers to celebrate everything from holidays to cherishing moments that were just ours and even some plain old regular days when he was thinking of me for no particular reason. I saved every tag that came with the flowers. I kept each card on the plastic stick that came with the flowers, and placed all of the cards in a vase so I had a collection. The vase sat on my kitchen sink. I read them as though they comprised my daily prayer book.

"Happy Fourth Anniversary. I love you," Steve.

"Just Because." Love, Steve.

"Happy Lust day. I lust for you." Love, Steve.

"The most important thing in life for me is spending time with you." Love, S.

"For all you do and for who you are...I love you

so much!!" Steve.
"I love you with all my heart, soul and physical being. Now and forever, 'til worlds split us apart."
Steve.
"Loving you is my greatest joy!" XOX Steve
"You are the sunshine of my life...Thanks for last night/morning." Steve
"You are always in my thoughts." Love, Steve
"Thanks for all the love and devotion." Steve
"Your smile brightens my day. Your love warms my heart." Steve
"My time with you is more precious than diamonds and gold." I love you, Steve.
"You make life worth living (not to mention fun!!!) Love you to bits." Steve
I took the card arrangement apart. The cards are in a drawer. I buy myself flowers now. It's not the same but it's the best that I can do.

I have been feeling physically lousy with a fever and emotionally with sadness for the past few days. I am very aware that my husband isn't around to take care of me when I'm sick. He was so attentive. One morning, I sat down and just started reading the cards he had given to me in the past for my birthdays. My birthday was just last week. Reality sank in that these were the last cards that I would ever receive. I have been crying and crying.

~Dee H.

Last night I pulled out the cards and letters that my husband wrote to me. I read them on my bed, one after the other. As I went along, I just cried. It's funny. I notice that my husband would write things like "Loving you 'til the end of time; I'll promise to give you flowers until I die; I long to grow old together with you; I'll sacrifice myself for you and our daughter." It sounds flowery but I know that he meant what he said.

~Connie N.

I made a little heart-shaped card for my husband. I wrote in it and stuck it in the niche, which is covered with marble. I allowed myself to cry profusely while cutting the card and selecting appropriate verses to write in it. I knew I had to release those pent-up tears. I felt better.

~Amanda P.

Sundays

*S*unday. 10:00 AM. *I've slept in. There is no reason to get up. We used to wake up together and snuggle. You'd make coffee and we'd walk to exercise. Then, we'd come back and read the Sunday paper. You had your Sports and Business sections. I had my Lifestyle, Travel, Home and Calendar sections. We read out loud, sharing our opinions, listening intently to each other. You cooked breakfast and I set the table with our favorite Sunday dishes. Oh, how I loved Sundays. You'd garden. I'd come out and admire your work. We'd sit and share the beauty of the flowers.*

Now I call Sundays, "Suicidal Sundays." I don't know how to flow anymore...alone...without you. I'm working on a plan to get through the day. I walk with my music. I cry a lot. I read the paper, even your sections and I wonder what you'd say. I eat different food and I never use the Sunday dishes. The phone doesn't ring. People are busy with their own lives. Suicidal Sunday is the hardest day of the week. I need a new plan.

It took me a year to find a plan for Sundays that wouldn't bring me back to my Sundays with Steve. I stopped

sleeping in, and I made myself busy with exercising, and work and chores that included the garden. I spent a lot of time in the garden, sitting, staring, thinking, and touching up, trying to keep everything perfect for Steve. I would weed the odd weed, clip the beautiful roses for my kitchen sink and cut a leaf off a plant that just didn't hang correctly. Roy, the gardener, had come to my husband's bedside the day before he died and promised Steve he'd keep the garden the way Steve liked it. I remember how he took off his muddy shoes, leaving them by the back door and quietly stood at the foot of the bed. I suppose this was unusual but Roy understood Steve's passion. The garden was so special to Steve and I wanted him to know that we would do everything in our power to keep it beautiful. Steve never opened his eyes but we knew he understood.

I obsessed over the garden. I used Steve's personal gardening calendar that marked all the fertilizing and pruning dates for the year. I organized all of the individual fertilizers in containers on the side of the house to make them easy to access. I made communication arrangements with Roy so he wouldn't miss a thing. My obsession focused me and gave me a reason to get up in the morning. I removed "suicidal" from Sundays. Grief was my companion on Sundays, but I grew to enjoy its company in a weird way. I knew I had to live the rest of my life and continue my journey. I found Steve in the shadows of Grief, and as time passed those shadows weakened and became dull.

It took more than a year before I mellowed, threw out the calendar and let Roy take over with his own fertilizers and plans. The garden will never be exactly the way Steve had it but it's beautiful and flourishing, and I know he approves.

Sundays are very lonely. Most of my friends are couples. I am working to make a simple life. The phone never rings on Sundays. I discovered how to take care of my emotional self. I make plans doing anything that makes me feel comfortable whether it's chores or gardening. If I get too lonesome by noon, I will call a single friend to go to dinner. I don't make advanced plans on Sundays because I don't know how I'm going to feel and sometimes hiding feels better.

~Rhondi R.

I hate Sundays, especially during football season, which starts in August and ends in late January. My husband watched football while I puttered around the house. He called me for every replay to explain what happened. I enjoyed our Sundays. Now they are empty. I don't like to turn on the TV. I'm afraid I'll run into football and the pain is too great.

~Earline F.

Sundays are time spent with my daughter and doing nothing else. She has gym class in the morning. This is not exactly a good time because it actually clashes with my church. Sundays are a day when most fathers participate. I thought that I should learn how to deal with this trigger. I might change the class to Saturday when I've conquered my sad feelings.

~Tracey O.

Today is Sunday. I have discovered that this is the day I perform every task that takes thought, frustrates me or that

I hate. I usually break the day up by visiting my sister, who has Alzheimer's. I love my home but Sundays are long, even in the house I love because my husband is gone and he made the house a home.

~Marlene A.

My husband of 30 years passed away eight months ago. We used to solve the Sunday crossword puzzle together. After his death, I couldn't read the paper anymore for fear that I'd come across an article he would have been interested in. I canceled our paper subscription. Now, eight months later, I am able to read the paper again.

~Bonnie S.

A Spouse's Personal Things

*Y*our wallet and your business telephone book are in your bathroom drawer. In all of the years we were married, I never looked through them or went through your desk drawer unless you asked me to get you something. These are your personal items. I'm not comfortable going into your drawers. If I open them up now, does that mean that you are really gone? I can't bear the thought.

I immediately gave the majority of your clothes to friends and family. I found comfort knowing that the people we cared about would wear them and carry you forward every day. I gave your ties to your colleagues. I don't want you forgotten. I gave your watches to two people you care so much about. Time is precious. They valued their time with you. Vice versa.

You'll never use any of those phone numbers again, nor the credit cards and driver's license. The people in your phone book will probably slip away. Business will move on without you. Can I?

That bathroom drawer remained closed for a year. When I finally cleaned it out, I cried and cried as I touched *and studied his things. I had always admired his handwriting, fine-tuned and elegant like him. I held his wallet next to my heart. I looked at his credit cards and driver's license that would never be used again. I no longer was a Mrs. to his Mr.*

Forms and applications had already been changed to reflect that I was now a Ms. or a W. Both made me cringe and choke. It was Steve's yearly pocket calendar that had the biggest emotional effect on me. He normally kept it in his briefcase but he had started leaving it in the bathroom drawer because of the numerous doctor appointments. I opened it slowly, staring at his handwriting. I sat on the floor reading his little notes in each dated square. The tears got heavier when I eyed the heart he'd drawn around our anniversary and my birthday. Steve's secret code for me was "LAW" and my initials were printed casually in many of the squares.

I placed the wallet and calendar in a safe place, hidden and out of the way. I took the notes and cards from other places and made a file called "Scrapbook," where his mementos sit to this day. It took four years to give Steve's glasses to a blind organization to reuse the frames.

Living without his smell lingering was the hardest to overcome. I kept his Polo cologne on his shelf, and dabbed it on my wrists when I got lonely. Sometimes, I put the cologne on his shirt and walked around the house wearing it. After a couple of years, though, the cologne went under the bathroom sink. I don't open it now but it's still there. I see it when I go under the sink to empty the trash. I feel a warmth and I smile. I can't, however, walk through the cologne section of the men's department store. No matter how happy I may be, the smell of Steve's cologne is emotionally too powerful for me. It is said that smells evoke the most powerful of memories...and gosh, are they right about that.

It's been just over three months. I was going through my wallet and I came across an envelope. My husband had written on the front, "Just because I love you." He had put money in the envelope when I was going with my daughter to a show in New York. I can't believe how seeing that envelope has thrown me back to the very beginning. How could this have happened to us? We never hurt anyone! We worked every day and took care of our business.

~Lianne V.

Although we had two bathrooms in our home, we often found ourselves in the morning needing to rush off for the day and sharing our comb. I liked looking in the mirror and watching my husband comb his hair. He never thought much of the texture of his hair. He said it was too curly and he had lots of curls. I, of course, coveted those curls. Over the years, I watched a little bald spot appear and then it grew larger. I loved that spot. As it expanded, so did our lives. It marked the years for us. When I comb my hair now, I use that comb. I haven't been able to part with this comb, his shaving brush, his razor and all of the objects that touched his face.

~Cecilia T.

My husband was killed in the capsizing of a 120-foot dive boat during a hurricane. I miss him so much that it causes me physical pain. We were married for 33 fantastic years and the years just kept getting better. We were going to retire in two years. He was 52 years old when he died and he was in excellent physical shape and health. He was into body building and his body was absolutely beautiful. I often go into the closet and smell his clothes, especially the robe that he wore in the morning after he left on his dive vacation. There is no smell that I can get. He always had the nicest skin, most beautiful body and the best smell. Now I can't get any of that and it's driving me crazy. For the first several nights after he died, I slept with the towel he used after his shower on that last morning. I am desperate to smell his things and get something of him from them. I just wish I had been on the boat with him. I should have been. I should have never let him go alone.

~Teri G.

My husband passed away a few months ago. Why can't I smell him in the house? It's like he hasn't even been here. Will he come to me and tell me that he is all right? I can take the fact that he is gone. But the smell is what I'm missing. He hadn't used after shave for eight years due to his disease. I feel so lost sometimes. Everyone said it will take time. But when I can't find the smell, it is like I lost him again.

~Annie Y.

It was very hard for me to pack all of my wife's clothes. It was almost three years before I could. I figured they weren't bothering me. I didn't need the room and I could look at the clothes and picture her in them. Some people would tell me to pack them away because I don't need these memories. I would say to myself, "That's all I have."

Well, I finally packed up her clothes but I couldn't part with them until recently. I have a dear friend at work who said that she would take the clothes and give them to people in need. She said that if she kept anything for herself, she wouldn't wear them to work where I could see them. After giving them to her, I thought how nice it would be to see someone making use of things that are so dear to me.

I told my friend it wouldn't bother me if she were to wear any of the clothes to work. Well, today she wore the raincoat that my wife bought when we were visiting England. I went up and hugged her and said, "Thanks."

It felt sad but it was a good feeling touching the coat and knowing that I can enjoy the memories.

~Dale D.

My wife passed away suddenly after our vacation in Paris. I put all of her clothes into the wardrobe and not a day goes by that I don't look at them, touch them and smell them. I miss her dreadfully. And for once, I cannot plan anything. Death is a good blocker of common sense. My days fly by and the nights drag. I look at the photograph of our family smiling on vacation three days before she died. I could never have imagined what awaited me when I returned. Just the smell of her clothes brings me to tears.

~Al P.

Last night, I lay on my bed facing my husband's side and calling his name as I pretended that he was sleeping. I kept asking him why he had to leave so early. Wasn't I supposed to have you longer? He kept his range of cologne bottles in the bathroom. I finally moved them to his closet drawer where his clothes hung. When I was in the study, I looked at the countless books he had and all the notes from his graduate courses. I wasn't prepared to throw them out although I do need to reorganize the shelves. I plan to keep them to show his daughter when she grows up.

~Sherrie R.

It's now a year since my husband died and I still have most of his things. I shove them around from drawer to drawer. His shoes are still in the closet as if he were going to put them on.

~Lachelle B.

Everything with his handwriting is in a drawer. Every once in a while I look at them and feel attached.

~Barbara S.

Part II

Venturing Out

Household Responsibilities

You *left with me so much to do alone. Not a day goes by that something you used to take care of needs my attention. I get tired of all the To Dos. It's not fair I have to do them all by myself now.*

> *Change the clocks on the outside lights and change the worn-out light bulbs.*
> *Change the sprinkler times on the clock.*
> *Figure out what is wrong with the plumbing in the toilet.*
> *What's that bug on the ceiling?*
> *Work with the gardener.*
> *Main fuse box? What are all those switches?*
> *Main water line? Where is it?*
> *Bank statements.*
> *Bookkeeping. Computers. All electronics. Cars.*
> *Errands. They still exist. They are just for one now.*
> *The house. EVERYTHING.*
> *It's all so overwhelming. We use to share it.*
> *Can I do it all?*
> *Can I do your half as well as you did?*

The day after Steve's funeral, getting out of bed was incredibly hard. I felt caught between being a dependent teenager who still needed her parents around for this and that, and a single, inexperienced adult who was flung into adulthood too soon. I wished for a guide, a "How to Live Alone," or something like that. All I had was instinct, and I suppose that's what got me out of bed, into the shower, out to the driveway for the paper and into the kitchen for breakfast. I still had to eat, bathe, pay attention to my bearings and get one foot in front of the other. Not even a ghost emerged to talk to me or give me guidance.

The car presented a huge problem when Steve died. I had spent so many years lying in the backseat of cars that I didn't have the opportunity to sit in the front seat and pay attention to a car's functions. Steve's '93 black Mercedes had been a compensation gift to him when we moved to Orange County for his new job. We both loved that car, our first luxury car. But it was a hassle to drive with its numerous gadgets and buttons. It didn't feel like mine when I was in the driver's seat. I learned only what I needed to learn to drive safely.

At first I made decisions that my dead husband would have approved of. Now I make decisions that work for me. I learned to be confident. I learned to develop new systems of living.

My first thought is I have all of the responsibilities. I need to drive so I can't have a drink. I need to buy the gift and sign my name alone. I will sit without my husband. It's painful watching others dance. It changes the tone of the occasion for me.

~Jeanna H.

My time is filled up with responsibilities I never had before. The biggest is the car. I can put the gas in my car but the car maintenance decisions are overwhelming.

~Rachelle M.

In the beginning, I was afraid to pump gas. I donned rubber gloves and steeled myself to attempt it. Now I laugh at myself. It was so very easy.

~Debbie H.

Now it really feels weird doing things like vacuuming, dusting and laundry. It still doesn't seem to be my job. That was always my husband's territory and he really enjoyed it. Gradually, it's getting easier to take everything on myself, including putting air in the tires and car repairs.

~Jeri P.

I have decided to move from my state to another state where our son lives. I have no family here now, but it was a really hard decision because of the many wonderful friends that helped me so much after my husband was killed. The house was absolutely full, and my friends did everything without even being asked. Even people at work that I really didn't know offered to help. It was absolutely amazing. I have been working very hard to get ready for the move. I have to make so many decisions that I don't know how to make but I make them anyway. I put the house on the market, signed a contract and it's closing this Thursday. Packing up was incredibly difficult. I thought I had prepared myself but it wasn't enough. I had been thinking about moving because this house is much too large for me but when the daffodils bloomed and they made me so sad, that was the final straw.

~Teri G.

First, I got a large yellow lawyer's tablet and started to make my list. It kept getting longer and longer. It took about two days to make. Sometimes I was choking and crying when I made the calls. I crossed off the calls as I made them, noticing right off the bat that there were different rules for women. We are treated like second-class citizens in the business world. Since I had always paid the bills and handled the budget, I carried that problem off well. The solution to this problem is for both the husband and wife to be included in running a household. It does not run by itself. It's important to keep each other informed in case of one party's death. It's important to have some knowledge about cars and upkeep. Know where and how to change fuses in the house. Know how to turn off the main power supplies and utilities. You must know this information because what was your man's job is now your job! Know where all the important papers are in the home and keep them organized.

~Mikki D.

I sold his truck to a friend. I see the truck all of the time and remembrances of him always pop up. It was his last bit of independence. If I could do that all over again, I would sell it to a stranger. Every time I see the damn truck, I think, there he is!

~Jennifer D.

Wedding Rings

$\mathcal{I}$ loved my wedding rings. They represented that I was special and that you chose me. I belonged and I was safe. I was loved and would never be alone again. I washed my rings once a week. I stared at them for 13 years in wonderment. You picked me. And then you left me.

A few months after my husband died, more pain of singledome hit me in the face. I believed if I moved my rings off my left hand, I was progressing through grief, which was so physically and emotionally consuming that it drowned me. I fought my grief by playing this game with my fingers, hoping that by controlling where I put my ring I'd be able to control the grief. I moved my engagement ring and wedding band to my right hand for a few minutes, then an hour, then weekdays. Every weekend, I moved them back to the wedding finger. Weekends were the loneliest. My friends were all with their spouses and children. I faced suicidal Sundays alone. But if I wore my rings, I felt safer and I belonged again.

Secure in my new living routine, I had the rings resized to fit on the middle finger of my left had. I put them on proudly and left the jewelry store only to come home, cry *hysterically, go back the next day and have the jeweler resize them for my wedding finger.*

Months later, my body told me it was time to move my rings. I practiced again. I moved the wedding band to the middle finger on my left hand and I moved the engagement ring to my ring finger on my right hand. They looked so lonely. I solved the problem by putting little bands on the front and back of each ring. I now felt that my rings had company.

I took my husband's ring and made it into a necklace. I feel very comfortable with this new setup. I wanted and needed to move my rings because in my social world, I am single and I need to remember that fact. I wear my rings and necklace every day. They still make me feel special and that I belong. And every now and then, when I'm alone at home, I put my original set back on the wedding ring finger of my left hand. Sometimes I cry, sometimes I smile but I always feel loved and not alone.

What we do with our wedding rings is a very personal issue for each of us. We didn't ask to be single. We are not divorced. I believe whatever we do in our timeline is right.

I am 27 going on 28 next month. About one year and five months after my husband's accident, I took off my wedding band and the engagement ring. I kept it in my drawer because I decided to release my husband to the Lord and close this chapter in my life. Closure doesn't mean to forget him. As for his ring, I actually got it back from the hospital when they gave me his belongings. I decided to wear it for him when he was embalmed and dressed up. I wore it and said to him, "We'll meet again in heaven" because I still very much wanted him to be my lifetime soul mate. Then I took the ring off and put it on his finger. He was cremated with his ring. After the cremation, I was told the diamond didn't melt but I never searched through the ashes to find it because my relatives suspected the cremators would have taken it and kept it for themselves. I could have used the diamond and made a pendant for my daughter in memory of her daddy. In hindsight, I have no regrets because I wasn't myself right after his death.

~Abby S.

I didn't remove my rings. I can't imagine why I would want to.

~Joyce S.

My fingers were swollen from arthritis and I couldn't wear my ring. I had to take it off and I felt unmarried. I hated it. It was bad enough that I lost him. I didn't want people to look at me and think I wasn't married because I still felt married. When the arthritis medicine took effect eight weeks later, and the swelling subsided, I immediately put on the ring and felt joyous.

~Janis S.

I have not removed my rings and have kept them on the same finger as always. I really have no intention of taking them off, ever. I still feel that we are married. Maybe that sounds crazy to some people, but it is the way I truly feel. This ring is special because he gave it to me for Mother's Day. It has rubies and diamonds. He absolutely loved rubies and he really seemed to enjoy buying them for me whenever he could. He had always planned to buy a bigger ruby for me. Now that will never happen. For a while, I wore his ring on a chain around my neck. Later, I moved his ring to my right hand (of course it's too big, but I refuse to have it resized) and anchored it with a smaller ring to keep it on my finger.

~Kathe W.

Last week I sat in the car and cleaned the cookie dough from my rings. When I finished, I went inside to play cards and my diamond ring was gone. I was devastated. Several people helped me look and look. We tore the car and my purse apart. We looked on all of the steps I had taken getting into the building. I had had that ring for 50 years. I couldn't be without it now. Then I saw it! I had put it on my other hand! I can't imagine taking my rings off.

~Lana S.

Rings…mmmmmm! Such a dilemma! I still wear mine. I think about it all the time. I just can't take them off. I feel like I would be letting him down if I stopped wearing them. I'm not sure if someday I'll feel differently, but not yet. A widower in a group I had attended said he came home from the funeral and took off his ring. He said, "We're not married anymore." I envy his acceptance of the situation. In his mind, it was just a fact. I think it also depends on what you are looking for. If you are interested in a new relationship, it will be easier to remove or move the rings. I'm not interested. Some people think I'm not moving on, but that's my business. Maybe it's not healthy, I don't know. But right now, all I can do is what is right for me.

~Lauren S.

Today I have taken off my wife's ring. I have been wearing it, with my own wedding ring, on my ring finger, since the night she died. I told a lie. I took it off and put it on another finger when I did a marathon—the Sunday after the funeral. I then put it back on my ring finger for a few days.

Then I took it off my ring finger again and put it on another finger. My neighbor came over and we sat in the garden before taking my kids for pizza. En route, I realized that I had lost my wife's ring. I kept it to myself but I was distraught.

I told my friend on the way back. We searched. She found it in the garden. I was so relieved. I would have been devastated if I had lost it. I put it back on my ring finger.

Later, I put it on my right hand to a fatter finger for safekeeping. The problem was that the end of that finger started to turn white. It hurt so much. I came home and used water, olive oil and soap to get it off. Nothing was working and I got panicky! I was really desperate. Shit, I'm going to have to hack my finger off. After about an hour, it came off and my finger was red raw, not white anymore. Subsequently, both rings got back onto the ring finger. And there it has stayed, on my ring finger, next to mine, until today, nearly three months after my wife's death.

I have really anguished over taking it off. I have asked a couple of people about where I should wear it. My mom said I should always keep it on my ring finger; I was married for life. I mentioned her opinion to my friends the other day. They said it was up to me, though one friend said many people wear it on a chain. Why have I made this so complicated?

I have really questioned why I want to take it off. Do I not want to send messages to single women that I am married? Probably there is a part of this in me, but the whole relationship thing is, well…I don't want to be in a relationship. I think, at least as much, that I don't want people to assume I am married, and in a "normal" relationship. No! My wife has died actually, and it was horrible, and there's just the three of us left and it's hard!

Anyway, today it made the journey to my little finger of my right hand. My own ring is on the ring finger of my right hand. This arrangement might work out.

~Jeff P.

I have been widowed for one year and three months. Shortly after the anniversary of my husband's suicide, I took off my wedding rings. Somehow this gesture seemed to reinforce my emerging image as "just me" without my beloved husband. We had been married 26-plus years at the time of his death, and his suicide was a completely unexpected event in my life. Around two months later, I looked at my rings in the jewelry armoire he had given me and I thought, "I need to put the rings back on. I am never going to be "just me; he will always be a part of me." I told my best friend that I had put the rings back on and she commented, "I guess you're not through being married to him yet." That is true. Maybe someday I will feel single, but I'm not there yet.

~Ellie M.

Walking Down a Crowded Street

I missed you today. I was walking down a crowded street trying not to get bumped in my back. I had to drag an airport carrier to carry my packages at the store. I had to use the handicap button on the side of the building to open the door for me. It swings by itself. I only go to big department stores now with automatic doors. I walk on the streets when it's less crowded because you are not there to protect me. You used to hold my hand, sometimes stop just to kiss me.

I saw an older couple today crossing the street at the crosswalk. I thought about us and how we had planned to grow old together, and that plaque in the garden that says, "Grow old along with me. The best is yet to be." It's all a lie. We read that poem at our wedding. John Lennon sang it. It doesn't matter if I am on a crowded street or alone on the street; I feel alone and never safe. You are not with me here and you are not waiting for me when I return.

It took a year before I could walk down a crowded street and actually see people. It took that long before I saw *people on the sand at the beach or saw them as I passed them on my walk. They were bodies and they had no faces. Sometimes I waved, sometimes I made a plastic smile as I scooted by, sometimes I just looked away. I didn't look for my husband in a crowd. I only felt him at the water's edge.*

I always wore a wedding band and walked through crowds alone but not really. I took comfort and pride in letting the world know I was married. After my husband died, physical problems caused my fingers to swell and I can't wear my rings anymore. I walk down the streets now and I look down at my finger that yells to the world, "She is single" and it breaks my heart.

~Lisa M.

After my 27-year-old son died, I saw him everywhere. He had bright red hair and a turned up nose. I looked at every red-haired man in a car believing it was him. The tears would well up. Every red head reminds me of him.

~Hy S.

I feel sad when I see other couples of any age walking or shopping together. I think how lucky they are.

~Robin J.

I shun crowds of any kind. It's just too painful.

~Jason P.

I miss those times we would walk down a street holding hands. I still think about this each time I have lunch and watch other couples stroll by. My mind just gets so filled with those happy memories, that at times, the tears start to flow. It's so painful but I just force myself to move on.

~James S.

The first thing that comes to my mind when I see other couples walking down the street is how alone I am. I miss the tall strong man to my right, my protector who made sure that I wouldn't get hurt by traffic or people. I miss the hand to hold, the arm around my waist or on my shoulder. The tears just flow thinking about it. I miss the human touch, my husband's touch. My protector. He is gone!

~Lizzie R.

It was extremely hard on the second anniversary of his death to get a phone call early in the morning and hear a voice say, "Hi, can I speak to your husband, please." It was such a light hearted happy voice and for a split second I was back at our home and about to reach the phone out to him and call, "Honey, phone for you." Then I realized in a shaky voice I had to tell this person that my husband died two years ago. Having had his own business made it hard for everyone to know that he died. It's moments like this that can still shock me with the reality of his absence. I still feel shock when I see his work vans driving around the town. I constantly am looking for him and this has been going on for a long time. Sudden death like my husband's is so cruel because you never get to say goodbye.

~Martha M.

I still have dreams where I'm saying to myself that I must miss my husband because I haven't heard from him in ages. Sometimes I'm in a crowded place and I'm looking for him but I just can't find him.

~Norienne P.

Hearing or Seeing Spouse's Name

I loved your name. I loved the look of it on paper. I would write Mrs. Steven S. Weis and smile. I kept your business card in my wallet. Pride. Confidence. Humble. My husband. I loved the sound of your name. One syllable. Steve. Strong. Safety.

I never went back to my maiden name. I had been married once before Steve, and was Laurie-Ann Mann when we met. At the time, I still had a hard time with all religions, especially Judaism because of the anti-Semitism that I had felt throughout my life. Yet, I was connected to God and that was enough. God and I had a special relationship and God had brought Steve and me together. I told Steve early on that his last name was the worst part about him. I didn't like the name "Weis" because of its exposure. I wanted to keep Mann. I wanted to remain disconnected to any single religion. But he told me that Weis with one S was German, and that Weiss with two S's was Jewish, so no one would bother me. Steve had also been raised Jewish, but had come to separate

95

religion from a private relationship with God. We kept many Jewish traditions when raising Jennifer, his daughter from a previous marriage, but we snuck in a few Christian elements as my mother had done—like Santa Clause and the Easter Bunny. I taught Jennifer that religion was merely a pathway to God. I drew an upside-down V and put God at the top.

"Religion is all of the trails to God at the top," I told her. "It doesn't matter how you get there as long as you don't tell others that they must be on your trail."

I've come to love Weis as my last name and can't picture myself ever changing it again. Weis is who I am. It's part of my identity. It also keeps Steve alive.

At first, just talking about him was a necessity. I wanted to hear his name. It's been one year and I still feel that way. When people talk about him, I feel like he's still real and exists. I want him to be remembered and talking about him keeps him alive for me.

~Paula S.

In the beginning, I simply cried whenever and wherever I heard his name. All of my embarrassment seemed to be nonexistent. I cried openly and sometimes uncontrollably. When I hear his name now, and it's been four years, I feel warm and connected and even, sometimes, irritated because solicitations still keep coming in my mailbox and on my telephone.

~Mary H.

Sometimes when I read his name on the e-mail or papers, it suddenly jolts my memory of him again and I just pause a little to think about him, before resuming reading my mail or the paper. I have to make myself snap out of it or I can't work clearly.

~Maureen S.

We played a game with the dog called "Get Daddy." "Give Daddy a kiss." I just can't say that name to our dog. She looks and looks for him to come home.

~Margo Y.

Hearing his name spoken within our family gives me comfort. I don't want anyone to forget him. He influenced so many people with his silly antics. He made us laugh and he could make us mad! He was quite a unique individual.

~Merry E.

I think, yes, that's his name but where is he? He needs to respond. I remember once, two sales people came to the door and asked to see the man of the house. They said his name. I said in such a hateful way, "Yes, I would love to see him, too, but he is dead, dead! Go to the cemetery and there you will see him!" I slammed the door full of hatred. Such insensitive people. Was I turning into a royal bitch? I wonder how other women handle these situations. Surely, not like I had just done.

~Denise S.

Dreams

There's little shelter in my dreams at night, for I have had one nightmare after another since seeing the black hole that your cancer put in your back. The vision haunts me and shakes me out of sleep night after night. I beat myself up emotionally because I had prayed over and over for God to take you or heal you but not let you suffer. And although you are finally pain-free and my wish has come true, I feel so depleted, so vacant, and just totally empty. I am the one suffering now. I am a shell and there is nothing but coils of pain inside. I want you back.

No matter what level of calm I found before closing my eyes, the nights always took hold of me. I'd awaken in flashes, my linens damp and my white t-shirt molded to me like a second skin that didn't quite fit. I'd sometimes awaken with unknown fear, terrified to come to my senses but desperate to understand and be back to normal. Those who've been around me when I sleep tell me that I cry out and fly upward as if possessed by a bad spirit. All the pain and sadness and fear that the daylight hours can't touch, would get worked out in the night.

None of my callings carried intelligible words. I wasn't being chased. I wasn't being abused. I wasn't climbing endless stairs or running down an infinite hallway. None of my cold sweats came with a heat wave in my room. Fear was all that seemed tangible. And in that fear came a great feeling of being lost. Lost in my nightmares, lost in myself.

The first ten months I would think about him all night. It wasn't really a dream. I would just have conversations with him. On the one-year anniversary of his passing, I had trouble falling asleep. When I finally fell asleep, I thought someone was making love to me. It was all the emotion that had died. I woke up and realized he had been making love to me in my dream. It was so real. I tried to go back to sleep so he would stay with me. It didn't work and it made me very sad but it felt good to have him there.

~Kim K.

I had a lot of dreams. I dreamt one night that I felt my husband's body next to me. I reached over and stroked the full image and outline of his nice, warm, comforting body. I thought to myself that he is here. Yes, he is. "It's you. You have come back to me!" It was so real, so real. In my mind and thoughts, I do believe he did come to me that one night.

~Madeline K.

I have been a widow for six years but the past few months I have had my husband in my dreams. These dreams are so vivid and now are actually quite comforting. Life does go on…a fact that I resented at first. We just keep going. I think it would hurt our partners if they knew the pain we have. We go through good days and bad.

~Stefanie W.

One year after my husband passed, he visited me. He woke me up and kissed me. He told me everything would be fine. I spoke to a counselor about this and he said this was normal. God allows these things to happen. It was not a dream. I do not dream and I'm not a nut case.

~Arlene S.

I dreamt that my wife was sitting upstairs in our living room making something for the kids like a puppet on a pencil. She was sitting there quietly putting the puppet together when she said, "Hee hee." She was acknowledging that she had finished and made a good job of it. This was so my wife. It was so us—our family. I was swimming in it. While in the dream, I remembered that it was my wife's birthday and I had to get her something and quickly. Panic! Then suddenly I realized that she was dead.

~Elliot R.

Last night I dreamt that my wife and I were in a really nice and friendly coffee bar. She was having a coffee asking for some strange cake, which I had never heard of. She was saying "Mmmmm, it is lovely," and raising her eyebrows. We were alone and indulging our time.

In the dream, I knew she was going soon; she couldn't

be with me for long because she was dead. It was still nice. I've had three dreams since my wife died, which made me happy because I was always annoyed before she died that I couldn't dream about her. So now, I dreamt about her and although it made me happy, it still made me sad. I can't recall every detail but I do know that she couldn't stay long.

~Paul S.

My husband had a massive heart attack in the passenger seat of my car. I was trying desperately to get him to the hospital when it hit him and though he "survived," if you can call it that, all of his organs failed. He never spoke another word and three days later, I had to have him unplugged.

A few months later, I had a dream that I was sitting on the couch and I looked over and he was sitting in a chair in the room and he grabbed his chest. I pulled up into a fetal position and started shaking all over and rocking and saying over and over, "Oh God, it's happening again..." My husband got up and walked across to me and sat down beside me. He wrapped his big, strong arms around me and whispered to me that everything was all right; he was all right. I felt so secure and warm and as I calmed down, I knew beyond any doubt that he really was all right where he was. When I woke up the next morning, I had such a peace about him that I knew he had visited me in my dream to let me know that he was okay and that I was going to be also.

~Kathleen H.

New Vocabulary Word: Widow

*Y*our escape from this world left me with a moniker I can hardly endure. It's not fair that I have to live with this new description of myself. I don't know if I'll ever marry again and claim the word "married." It's strange to think that you were a widower when we met. You didn't play the part and didn't encompass that word at all. You had been freed by your first wife's long illness and the personal struggles that led to her death. I saw you as a vibrant, independent, strong, compassionate...single man when you arrived that day to speak with me about your daughter's tutoring. I wonder if I will I ever feel vibrant, independent, and strong like that? Will I ever be able to ax the word "widow" from my profile or at least be comfortable with it? Maybe I can just go back to pretending I am single. But maybe that's too youthful of a word. I supposed those who are labeled as "divorced" have similar issues. It's as if society marks you in some way to show the world that you're tainted goods. Single = young. Married = normal. Divorced = experienced (in a negative way). Widowed= tainted, old, sad.

The word "widow" makes my body choke. Widows are to be feared. Widow is a black spider that I killed as a child. Widow is a woman who is left in tragedy. It's a scary word and it scares people away. On applications, I must now check the box with W. I'm in a new category. The person who reads it gives me a pitiful look. Sometimes they say, "I'm sorry." Widow doesn't mean "single" in a healthy way. It screams "tragedy, sadness, pain." It means you're not invited anymore or if you are, a guest is rarely—if ever—included. Widow means others in the future will wonder if they can ever live up to or not be compared to your lost love. Widow is a sentence that you carry forever in your heart.

The word widow is a reality I don't like but the word itself doesn't bother me. Ms bothers me because it takes away the fact that I'm not a Mrs. It's almost like my marriage didn't exist.

~Dorothy R.

The word widow didn't dawn on me until it was time to inform major organizations of my husband's death. I had to fill out a multitude of forms indicating my present marital status: widowed! I felt ostracized from the community because it's very rare to hear this word, especially when I am so young. I felt so upset that I was somewhat demoted from the status of being "married" to "widowed." I also felt embarrassed to tell people I am widowed. In a nutshell, this word is just awful to use. If there is an option for widow, I'll just skip it and check "single" instead. It isn't wrong to call ourselves single because we are! Fellow widows have told me it's better being widowed than divorced because that latter means your husband couldn't stand you while the former means your husband died but he still loved you. That's my consolation but still, I am not using this term.

~Lynn Q.

Oh how I detested that word. I just did not know what I was or who I was at that time. I went to church and I was given a form to fill out. It had a selection of titles. I had to ask my neighbor, "What am I?" Isn't that just so sad? I felt so alone like I was a nobody and a nothing. I was like an eggshell with innards sucked out of the main part of the egg. Now I'm just a shell of a woman, alive with no meaning, no purpose, unwanted and a nuisance. Here come more tears, a lump in my throat and I'm swallowing hard. Gulp! Who am I? Darling, why did you leave me here? I need you now as my protector. Tell me what and who I am? I don't know. I don't know. How awful. The pain, the pain.

~Rebecca N.

"Zc" in Yiddish is sweet. I still hear my Zc at the door. I haven't had a hug in seven months. Getting used to "widow" is rough.

~Francis D.

I'm new at this. About a month after my husband's death, I went to a lunch with his high school graduates of 50+ years. I was introduced as his widow. I said, "I hate that word. I'm not a widow." "Well, then what are you?" "I'm his ex!" No, they decided that I couldn't be that. So what am I? Who am I?

~Becky D.

To this day, I haven't used the word, "widowed." People still call and ask if they can speak to my wife. I just say, "Sorry, she is not here," and I hang up. It will be three years on the 15th of this month so I know that whoever is calling her didn't know her.

~Richard M.

I have learned never to use the word "widow" in reference to myself. When sales people call and ask for my husband, I think that I don't have a husband anymore and I get very sad. One day, I shouted at a poor fellow at the other end of the phone, "He is deceased. Take his name off your list." That felt better. This was all about his leaving me. He had the name "deceased." I am not going to deal with a new title. Now I just shout at the phone and feel better.

~Sandra G.

I've had to check that "widow" box several times since my husband died. The first time was at a doctor appointment and it was like a physical stab to my chest to have to do it. Now I look at it much differently. I check that box almost with a feeling of pride because I really am proud to be his widow. I can claim that and no one else can. Now it makes me angry when the only boxes are married, divorced or single. I usually draw in my own box simply to make a point and make them think about the need for a form revision.

~Stephanie W.

The first night without him I woke up and thought, "I am a widow." I do not want to be a "widow." I want to be married, a wife. It was really frightening to be confronted by this and there was no way that I could escape.

~Susan H.

Hi! How Are You?

*T*he only reason I answered the phone after your death was so I could dream that you'd call and let me know you were okay, and that you didn't really die. But you never called.

You were so good about calling me when we were married. You'd check in with me a few times during the day to see how I was doing and to send your love. The times you called for no particular reason other than to say hello and say "I Love You," were my favorite phone calls. And the times you'd call while driving up our street on your way home got me all fired up for the night or, if it was a Friday, for the entire weekend. You were an incredibly busy man, and you had to deal with dozens of people under your command every day, and yet you still found time to call me for a quick hello. I'll never forget the first time you called me after we met—it was from an airplane back when airphones were so new to flights and prohibitively expensive! For a man who was overall reserved and quiet, you were excellent when it came to communication and calling "just because." You never even used the words "how are you," because you were so much more creative and deeper than that.

The phone rings. The person at the other end says, "Hi! How are you?" or "How do you feel?" I would hear those words and want to flush the words with the person down the toilet! I would sarcastically think, how am I? Get a clue! I hate that you are asking me that as you are driving in your car while talking on the cell phone with your normal life.

Sometimes I want you to call and sometimes I don't. The fact is, you can't win. I know deep down you really don't want to hear the truth. My pain hurts you and you feel helpless. I want it all to go away but I don't have that power. You are also secretly glad that this hasn't happened to you and I am a reminder that it can.

So I lie and say, "I'm fine." Sometimes I just can't control myself and cry, forcing you to be stuck with my choking and tears. But I'm glad that you called and that you care. I'm glad that you made my phone ring. Widowhood means the phone rings fewer times. And truly, I am so glad that you don't understand my pain. It means that you have never been through this. Thank you for calling.

"How are you?" are the worst words that you can ask me. In fact, I finally told a relative, "Please don't ask me how I am every day. I'm the same as I was yesterday."

~Tina B.

I simply say, "Okay" or "Well, thank you." People in general cannot understand loss. If it is someone who knows me well, I might answer, "A little down today."

~El S.

I hated this question very much because my question in return would be, "How do you think I am as I've gone through a horrible patch?" I really wished the person who asked could be more sensitive to my feelings. But I summed up that they, too, are probably lost for words when they see me so this was probably a natural question to ask. I still get this question and my clichéd answer is, "I am fine, thank-you." And for closer friends, I say, "I am coping in a painful way but getting there."

~Winifred W.

I know people mean well when they ask, "How are you?" I just say, "Fine." What else can we say? If you say, "I'm lonely," most of them say, "You have to let go and move on. You still have a lot to live for like your kids and grandkids. You will meet someone and be happy again." How am I? Some days seem like they will never end. On other days, I don't want to leave the house we spent so much time together in. People say things will get easier. A few people say, why don't you retire and travel? That would be fun—traveling alone! Sometimes I say, "No, they don't get easier. You just learn to live with it." We do learn to live with it because we have wonderful memories to keep us going.

~Elwin F.

It occurred to me that I didn't really talk about the period of grief when people stopped to talk to me. They felt too awkward to say anything because they didn't want to upset me so they said nothing. I also remember my "flippant phase" when people used to stop me in the street and tell me how sorry they were that I had lost my husband. I would say,

"Yes, very careless of me!"

Honestly, I'm not really so horrible, but at that time I wanted people to feel uncomfortable because I felt so badly.

~Marge T.

I pretend a lot and I have become a pretty good actress. After all, you feel people don't want to see a sad grieving face all the time or hear anymore about what you are going through or feeling so you get good at pretending and saying everything is going okay. Only it's not. I am so lonely. I am one of those "old fashioned women" who lived with her parents until I got married at age 23. I had my son at age 24 (yes...after 10 months) and my daughter two years later. Ten years later, we had another daughter. I now have six grandchildren and they are the light of my life. But I am still alone and feel alone even when family and friends are around me. But I can't let them see that or know that because society is uncomfortable around people in mourning.

~Amy E.

How are you? Sometimes I wonder if anyone really expects to get a truthful answer to this question. How are you doing? "Okay" only translates to: I am miserable, lost, scared, lonely, brokenhearted, hopeless. I want to yell out these things, but with a small voice I simply say, okay or I am making it...what do they want to hear? Not the truth. Every second is a struggle, to eat, to sleep, to breath...to live. I feel like I am in a really dark hole looking to the sky but I see no light. I never have experienced such hopelessness. The future only looks empty.

~Catherine Z.

Coming Home to an Empty House

I'm not sure what to wear. I'm going out and I want to show you two outfits so you can pick. I decided on one outfit and I'm standing in front of the mirror empty hearted. You would always say something nice like, "You look beautiful" or "I like that outfit on you." I look but I have no words. I feel nonexistent. It doesn't matter what I wear. It was fun to dress up because it made you smile.

I leave. I go through the motions of the evening with my fake smile. I realize during the evening that it doesn't matter when I come home. The house is empty. I'm glad that I left a light and television on. At least when I open the door, there will be noise to fill the dreaded silence. You are not there to share my thoughts. We used to call it "Update" and compare notes.

I climb into bed and turn off all the lights. I watch familiar faces on the television as I cuddle with my comforter in the dark. I'm safe again in my home but so empty.

It took me a long time to get used to living in my own skin and knowing that Steve wasn't there to confirm how I looked. I eventually was able to get dressed by making my own choices and feeling good about them. I put on make-up without crying. I left lights on for my own personal security, but not always the television. I called a girlfriend when I got home, and learned to reconnect with myself. The house is no longer empty.

This is still and probably will always be awful. Loneliness and not being able to share the everyday happenings continue to be difficult to deal with. It is the worst when all the chores are done.

~Leah M.

The house makes so many unexplainable noises when you are in the house alone. You can't blame the thump on your mate when he or she is gone. Also, who is getting this house so dirty? I live alone and don't have that much company. The messes and clutter...good grief.

~Geri H.

I have been alone for almost one year and it feels like forever. I am going to counseling and I told the counselor that I felt like an egg, insulated from the world. Even in my own home, I feel like an egg.

~Zida M.

There is no greeting. "Honey, is that you?" or "Dear, is that you?" I miss the terms of endearment. My name, my name. His voice, his manly voice that tells me I am his wife, his beloved. He missed me. I love the warm feeling inside me that I knew he really cared about his woman. No kiss, no embrace. No hug. No nothing! Nothing! Emptiness is alone! You are all alone! Who cares? No one but you! You flop onto the couch or chair and cry. Every time it's the same thing.

~Ellen R.

I feel peace to finally be back in my own home. I guess having stayed with my in-laws for four months after my husband died made me treasure my home much more. Of course, there are times of loneliness, especially when I am tending to my daughter. I pray to God and share with him my pain and tears. I feel comforted by his peace.

~Shelly W.

I want to get away from myself and there is no place to go. It's only been five weeks since my husband died. I wish I could leave my body to escape the horrible feeling of pain and anguish. My husband was a fun loving guy. No one could ever make me laugh like he could. I know he would say, "What's the matter with you? Do what you want to do...go on." The problem is all I ever did was for him or for us. I never thought about me.

~Bella W.

Some days seem like they will never end. Some days I don't want to leave the house we spent so much time together in. When I go to my son's and daughter's houses, it's hard to leave knowing I am going home to an empty house with nothing to do but think of memories.

~Christine S.

My family always tries to ensure that my daughter and I get home safely. I have become so dependent. I feel so embarrassed that I have become such a burden. I hate that feeling.

~Naomi T.

I can't tell you how hard it is to unlock the door and open it and see everything is still in the same place where I left it. I don't hear a "Hi, honey. I hope you are hungry" or "So how was your day?" The empty feeling that runs through my heart is so deep I want to just run out and not come back until she does. The house is so big to me but I still feel the love that my wife and I had here. That's what keeps me from not running. I believe that's why she did not want to come home and die here. She wanted me to remember the love we had here. I would walk in the door and say, "Hi honey. I am home" and to this day, I still do. I would give anything just to hear her voice one more time.

~Tom D.

Part III

Social Consciousness

Invitations for One

*D*o you remember the time we were invited to our first formal dinner dance? I didn't have an appropriate dress. You took me to Saks and combed the formal wear racks with the sales lady. You helped me into the dressing room and asked me to try on that purple dress. I blushed with embarrassment. I shook off my jeans and t-shirt to slip on an Oleg Cassini, slim-fitting, sequined purple dress. I felt like Julia Roberts in "Pretty Woman." You smiled and said I looked beautiful. I was so painfully shy about my sexuality when I met you. I felt comfortable only in my Birkenstock sandals, blue jeans and sweats. I had very little self-confidence trying on a sexy dress or the confidence to purchase one, let alone wear it out in public with you by my side.

But you, oh you, with your dazzling eyes and soft words said that I could wear anything and look beautiful. You opened the door to dressing up and feeling pretty. To make it easy for me, we played a game called Outfit A-B-C. We would receive an invitation and choose an outfit. When we got home, we'd rip them off and get back into our jeans or sweats. I could go anywhere with you.

I didn't accept invitations easily the first year. It was too painful to get dressed alone, go out alone, walk in alone and sit alone watching other couples. I had no skill in making "cocktail" conversation. I had a small circle of close friends and they were the center of my universe. I spoke with them mostly on the phone and went out alone in the daytime to the beach and on errands. I had one girlfriend who helped me learn to drive to new destinations alone. Eventually, I began to accept invitations in the daytime from people who cushioned my arrival. I got dressed three or four times before I could feel confident about attending. They made sure that I wasn't alone at the event. Sometimes, I didn't talk but at least I went. Accepting evening invitations came much later.

Eventually, I learned to stay in the present with my feelings and enjoy pleasurable moments of events. I even started to like meeting new people. However, as I walked out the door, alone, my heart would always momentarily sink. It was pure reality that I was an invitation for one but I was proud of myself for attending. I didn't want to be isolated anymore. I was moving forward.

Invitations for one are just a constant reminder that you are alone in this world. If you do decide to go, you see how all of the couples are dancing, kissing, holding hands, having eyes only for each other. You get an ache that no pill or special concoction can take away. I would say to myself, "We did that. We loved like that. We kissed that way. You held me in your arms and took my breath away!" The emptiness we feel shows on our face. I do not want pity. I think about someone coming along to hold me, hug me and make these horrible feelings end. "Why did you have to die? Don't you know you were my life, my love, my only love? You were all that I had!" I did put all my eggs in one basket. "My Love, visit me in my dreams tonight. Hold me, just hold me tight and say it is all a dream." But it's a nightmare! I wake up and the bed has only me and my teddy bear. I am a little girl lost! The woman inside is an empty shell, never to be whole again.

~Isabella F.

۷

My very first invitation for one was to a wedding in a far-off location. I had to stay in a hotel so I invited two girlfriends to stay with me while I got dressed so I wouldn't feel so alone.

~Danielle C.

۷

I have declined all invitations so far. I can't take parties and big events. It pains me that my spouse is no longer with me. We enjoyed functions and parties very much. We both would dress up. Now I don't. Life is plain and simple for me. I intend to keep it that way for another year or so.

~Lori G.

۷

An invitation for one is the most annoying thing that I ever received. A family member (on hubby's side) sent me a wedding invitation "for one" with no "and friend." They were aware that I was close to hubby's best friend yet they still expected me to travel 10 hours away for a weekend wedding with or without my three kids and not take a companion. How bloody rude! Do they think I am no longer a female with needs for companionship? I decided not to go. My mother-in-law replied for me. I would not go to a wedding by myself. The only people I would know would be the groom's family who I presume would not spend the evening keeping me company. I would have felt terribly out of place.

Eighteen months later I received another invitation for one for a wedding from the same family. It was addressed only to me.

~Elaine A.

I met my husband when he asked me to join his band as a singer. After a while, our personal relationship ended and I left the band. We got back together eight years later and I became his wife. I was reunited with people whom I hadn't seen for a long time. The years that we were separated were wiped away and we all got along so well.

When my husband died, after these people had "paid their respects," I stopped getting invited because I was a single woman! The wives didn't like that, or even worse, some single geek guy would just happen to be invited, too (barf!).

~Elizabeth M.

It's been 18 months since my husband died and invitations still come with just my name. Is it because people just don't realize? Is it a catch-22 situation? What is the correct way to do this? I guess if I was on their end, I may be stuck with the same dilemma. It seems to me that because people don't know what to say, they just don't say anything. Phone calls stop, visits stop, and then you get the real fools who pretend not to see you in the street and cross the road just so they don't have to confront their own fears. Strange, I guess.

I wonder how I would have reacted. I can't ever remember meeting a widow or widower, but perhaps I have.

~Jan R.

Celebrations, Holidays and Birthdays

Silently, I knew it would be your last Christmas with me. The holidays now had no celebration. They were just an awareness that you wouldn't be here with me anymore to celebrate anything. I couldn't decorate for you. The den was filled with your hospital bed and other items of survival. This broke my heart because you loved the way we decorated. You loved the music, the food, and the laughter. It was all gone. Sharing all of the holidays with you gave the holidays meaning. You were so sick but you were aware of everything that was happening. Because you loved California poppies and planted them each year, I bought a large statue for the garden of a cherub holding a poppy over his head. I put it in the garden so you could look at it through the window from your hospital bed. I still don't know if that was the right or wrong thing to do. Presents didn't matter anymore but I knew it was the last present that I could ever buy you. I was self-indulgent. I had to buy it for you because I loved shopping for you and I knew it was over.

New Years followed. You were barely coherent. I knew the end was close. I sat by your bed and read to you. I talked to you as you slept and you went some place in your head that I couldn't go to. The tears dripped down my cheeks as I touched you. You smelled like death but I didn't care. Eight days later, you died, and the holidays with all their celebration, died with you.

The first year following my husband's death was unbearable but the holidays were beyond unbearable. I was numb and saying that I was severely sad can't even describe it. I had friends and family that remembered me during the holidays and celebrations. They sent me flowers and cards, and called me leaving very nice messages. Flowers reminded me of the funeral. The cards made me cry. No one could help me. I was in an unreachable zone of despair but the contact was good for me, even though I didn't know it then. I went to Hawaii with my mother for Thanksgiving. I couldn't face another holiday in my house without Steve. But I was too broken-hearted to enjoy Hawaii. I cried a lot and my sadness was not good for my mother who was in her own mourning for her son-in-law. After seeing what I was like, I spent Christmas alone, at the beach, where I felt that I could feel Steve and God. I turned down all invitations.

I remember thinking on New Year's Eve that I had made it to some degree just by getting through the first year of mourning. It was the eve of the new millennium, and I barely noticed. I sat on the couch eating frozen almonds and watched the taped celebrations from around the world on CNN, breathing calmly through the quiet transition between '99 and '00. I had arrived in this new year, a new side, and would find a way to get through another year. "Let's make it a better one," I said to myself.

The second year was very different. People had their

own lives and the numerous cards stopped coming. I had a close circle of friends that always remembered. However, I spent the holidays alone, which was always my choice. I couldn't handle being with families. One particular girlfriend called on every occasion just to say she was thinking of me. To this day, she still does, and it feels good.

Every holiday or anniversary in year three brought a great depth of pain to me. Sometimes, I made it through the day and evening without shedding a tear only to fall apart the next day and be depressed for two more days. Other times, I'd be so overwhelmed days before a special day anticipating its pain that by the time the actual day arrived, the pain had washed out of me.

By year four, I was able to attend events and not cry. I saw the sadness of not sharing come and go but it was manageable. I realized that I had to work hard to make any of it matter and I could only do this by celebrating others enjoying their day. I finally had something to give and I counted my blessings for that.

Holidays are the worst for me since my wife died. We always celebrated our birthdays on the exact date with the entire family. It became a tradition and even now, my children continue to celebrate birthdays on their birthdates. I still sign the cards with Grandma and my nickname.

Christmas was a big family event and everyone came to our house to open presents and have breakfast before they left to visit others. It's different now. We have Christmas at my son's house. It's nice seeing the kids unwrap their presents but it's sad. I feel alone with my family crowd around and it's hard to hold back the tears.

Everyone misses my wife. Her colleagues at work invite me to all of their celebrations. There will always be dates that remind us of our loss. Anniversaries, graduations, birthdays, etc. I smile because I know my wife will always be with me and she would want us to enjoy life, especially birthdays, for she gave me two beautiful children and five grandchildren.

~Shane B.

It doesn't matter if I am with family or friends, I feel out of place.

~Steven D.

I enjoy the children's birthdays. I feel so sad when I can't share the joy.

~Edna C.

Birthdays are sad to me because I am growing old alone.

~Diane C.

I was numb from caretaking for the first holiday that I experienced alone. The second year, I realized I was alone. I would have given anything to have him back, caretaking and all.

~Diana C.

On Thanksgiving, we toast him before the meal. Everyone says something about him. This is very comforting.

~Sadie G.

൙

Holidays are days like any other day. I spend them by myself. I am glad when they are over because the holiday season gets harder instead of easier.

~Janet M.

൙

This December was my first Christmas without my husband. Instead of going through our traditional list of names, I decided that I would only send cards to the people who sent me a card. I had no idea that writing my first card would be so difficult. When it came time to write our names, I froze. What do I do? Then it came easy but with tears. For the first card, I wrote both of our names with a note that explained that I had to write both names because he was here in my heart. The rest of the cards I just wrote my name but shed many tears.

~Diane H.

൙

I cringe each time I think I have to face a celebration without my husband. So far, I have faced my parent's birthdays and my birthday single. I didn't want to attend Father's Day but I had to because my father adores my daughter.

I try to avoid celebrations with my in-laws side of the family. It's just too hard without my husband. I feel awkward seeing my brother and sister-in-law as one intact family unit.

I did not attend my brother-in-law's birthday. My father-in-law plays favoritism with the grandchildren and my daughter is not at the top of his list. I just can't. I attended Mother's Day because I love my mother-in-law so much. It's sad and I have to face this horrible feeling all alone.

~Rose D.

I just felt down today. I had a birthday yesterday and they don't usually bother me but this one did. It just hit me that in a few more birthdays, I will actually be older than my husband was or ever will be. I don't know why, but I continue to be amazed by things like that.

~Sandra C.

Sundays and holidays were quite tough at first. My first Christmas without him was an ordeal. All of the family went to my sister's house. What sticks out in my mind from that day was that I was surrounded by people I loved and I felt like the loneliest person in the world. I had to wear a silly hat, pull crackers, and smile until my face actually ached. I kept remembering the times that my husband and I would do a funky chicken dance. We looked so daft but we made it our part of the traditions. Eventually, enough time passed to allow me to politely leave. I think that was probably the time I cried the most. Being back in our home gave me the freedom to cry and just not care, as there was no one to see.

~Jill G.

It was my wife's birthday. I thought it would be like a normal day. It wasn't. I didn't receive any cards for my wife, thank goodness. I was worried that I had forgotten to tell someone. I received a couple of cards about her, reminding me to think about all the great birthdays she had had, her beauty, and I also received some flowers. We had cake. Our children and I sang "Happy Birthday." I didn't make it to the end of the song.

~Ivan B.

Yesterday was the fourth anniversary of my husband's passing away. It still feels as sad as it has from day one. I had those flashbacks of scenes at the end, talking to him in the emergency room, holding him and feeling him take his last two soft breaths. He was only 61 and I was 57, but with this anniversary I am more aware of how time is flying by; how I am four years older now. Four years is a good chunk of time. I remind myself to try and live the rest of my life to the fullest and as best I can. We all should appreciate each day and even though my heart has a huge hole that no one can fill, I still try to find pleasure in life's offerings.

~Lorrie H.

I have so many feelings about holidays with a new partner.

Angry – she did not like some of the foods that my wife adored.

Alone – not having my wife there.

Defensive – about things my wife and I had done on holidays and enjoying them.

Responsible – for doing things: my wife was the big organizer, my new partner is not.

Guilty – for comparing her with my wife.

Selfish – they are my kids and it is me and them; can I let anyone in?

~Bob S.

A new year. It's bullshit. Why do things have to be this hard? Thought I was finding myself but all I am doing is losing myself. Losing myself in a web of alcohol and people who mean nothing to me. I am pissed at you. I sometimes can't do this. I went to see your family and rode around with your brother while he played this song that was about death. I missed you. I always miss you. But, being with family always makes me feel closer to you. Hugging your family feels good. I just wish you were there to hug instead. Your sister came over and we talked for hours, crying, listening to music, visiting your grave, smoking cigarettes, and drinking wine. We talked of things we should try, ice-skating with no ice, jumping out of a plane without a parachute, crossing train tracks without beating the train. Obviously at this point, we were talking about committing suicide to be with you, but it was a form of release for us and we were half laughing while we came up with new ideas. After she left, I laid on the floor and cried and cried and cried. The sobs are heart-wrenching and my whole body aches. The holidays have got to be the worst. It's supposed to be this time when you are happy and with family. Not for me.

~Lorna P.

You know, it's funny. Halloween isn't really a holiday but I missed my husband so much yesterday. I no longer pass out candy since he passed away but I have such memories of the both of us doing it together. He is wearing his warm flannel shirt, sitting on a chair, kidding the children when they came back for seconds. We would take turns as we tired. We always tried to guess who it was in the costume. Was this child one of our neighbor's children? Then we both would tease the little ones.

Waves of sadness came over me today and I said to myself that this is normal. We had shared this fun together so I let the few tears that I was holding back flow freely. I feel his presence so very much and it is comforting. Even in church, I can almost feel his arm around my shoulder. Last night, I just wanted to hold his hand and snuggle and cuddle like we did so many times through the years after a holiday and the day was over. I miss the playful times, the quiet times when we read each other's minds. I miss the times he would wait on me and bring me a warm cup of tea. I miss him rubbing my feet and now I massage my own feet and pretend it's him doing it. I know this sounds crazy but that's what I do.

~Alma F.

It's my wife's birthday today. I took roses to her, which I always sent to her on special days. She would always say people were surprised because their husbands never sent them flowers. It's just something I did but when I look back, it wasn't enough. It's going to be six years and the memories mean more every day.

~Brian L.

130

Yesterday was my wedding anniversary. It had so many sad moments. It went well overall. I was on a trip in another country. On our anniversary night, I had dinner with the Ambassador to my country so that event took my mind away from my anniversary. However, I had sent a text message in my phone addressing it to my husband, saying, "I missed sharing this day with you. I thought that I could live without you. I was wrong. It's been a struggle. Being in another country, traveling like we did, makes me wish you could be here with me. I miss the intimacy we shared together as a couple."

~Cheryl Q.

I've gone through a few more hurdles after the death of my husband due to cancer almost five months ago. I've faced what would have been our 41st anniversary, Thanksgiving, Christmas, New Year's, and his birthday, which would have been today, without him. It's sure been tough, but those "firsts" are, I think, the dreaded ones to face and I've done so all at once within five months. Good or bad, I don't know. I sometimes feel that I am on a very fast train and every holiday, anniversary or birthday is supposed to be a quick stop in a little town. But the train doesn't really stop. Is this how my life will now experience certain day events like a blur?

~Kelly F.

I'm getting used to a new life and a new way of living. I'm self-employed now. I'm taking care of the house, money, food and all of the stuff that needs doing. Holidays are just with the kids and me. Easter came soon after my wife's death followed by a long summer holiday. It was just us getting used to organizing, packing, and making arrangements with friends. Bloody Christmas. I have never felt so pressured and tired.

~Ron M.

~

Someone told me that anniversaries are worse than everyday life without your husband because everyday life is routine. You draw on strength. You put up your shields and crack on. When the anniversary comes, you don't expect the strength of your feelings. You haven't got the shield anymore. You are startled by your feelings. I think there may be truth in this.

~Heather M.

~

It's year two without my husband. Yesterday was my birthday. I keep asking myself if I was happy on my birthday without my husband. And the answer is yes. I feel different in year two. There is more joy, less tears. I feel that I can find my own joy without him. It's probably because I filled this day. That night, I did speak to my mom and we talked about him. I did tear. We were still discussing the disbelief of his sudden death, a tragedy.

~Shirlee Q.

~

I am kind of blue for Thanksgiving. It will be my youngest son's birthday, too. He will be 40 and he is getting married next April. I have been missing my husband terribly. I am so lonely for him. I am cooking a turkey dinner for my daughter and one son who lives with me. My heart is not in it. I will be so glad when the holidays are over with. The memories and the music are all getting to me.

~Lacey A.

My husband was a New Year's baby so we had that event to pass through right behind Christmas. I had written our children and grandchildren ahead of time and told them that it would be difficult. Some things we would have to change and others we would not change, but we would get through the holiday. Instead of chili and oyster stew, our usual meal, our oldest granddaughter and I went to Sam's (Wal-mart's discount store) and bought all the fun food that needed no preparation, just heating. My husband always read the Christmas story from the book of Luke so our oldest grandson was given that honor. Christmas carols were sung. Santa Claus (my brother) made his annual appearance (we still have one believer in the family) and gifts were passed out. Tears and all, I thought Christmas went quite well.

~Camile R.

Social Life: Returning Alone

I'm reinventing myself. I'm starting to do things I've never done before, like take singing and dancing lessons, and having frequent lunches with friends. I'm also going to seminars to keep up my education and learn new information. I even tried a seminar on magnets since we tried using them to heal you. It's weird packing for one and staying in a hotel room all by myself, but it's getting better. I'm growing.

One afternoon, I opened my mail and found an ad cut out by my mother that read, "It's Just Lunch." I called her immediately and she started talking about how I needed to practice getting dressed, going out, driving myself, and socializing with new people. As it turned out, "It's Just Lunch" is a dating service, so this was her way of saying I needed to start dating again.

Failure is not trying, Steve. You told me that yourself. And I believe it. I know I lack the skills a single woman needs to survive in this world. I need to get back that confidence if I'm going to survive at all. I know this. I also know that I can't take a moment for granted. We just don't know how long we have on Earth. I have a choice. I have lots of choices, but the greatest one is to choose to live and live well. I don't know if I trust that everything will work out, but I'll try. God has a plan for all of us, I think. I'll keep praying every morning that God will make my day safe and I'll do my best to get through that day with some joy.

So I got going. I wanted to get all of the firsts over as soon as possible. I planned to do everything well. I didn't want any lesson twice; they were too hard. And frankly, I didn't want to start these lessons of growth four, five, six years from now.

I called "It's Just Lunch," made an appointment and signed up for nine lunch dates. I bought Leil Lowndes's How to Talk to Anybody About Anything and started reading. I read lots of self-help guru books. The principles and perspectives that came through reading and learning from psychologists and authors helped me reinvent myself and my thought process. I knew that if I wanted joy again in its purest form, I'd have to make the choice. No one could give it to me. I'd have to look at joy as though it were an athletic competition. To have joy again at any level was a lot of work, like training for an Olympic event. Joy doesn't walk into a room by itself, like an athlete doesn't win a competition without serious effort and practice. I'd deal with the morning, the afternoon and then the nighttime hour by hour. I'd do something and try to stay right in the moment. There's joy in watching a student accomplish a word problem, reading a good story or enjoying a sunset for a brief second. I'd focus on the moment, recognize the joy and let it add up.

The goal was to have more joy in a day than sadness. It wasn't the same kind of joy I had shared with Steve; it was a joy I learned on my own with practice, for me and my own soul. When I was sad, the next goal was getting out of that sadness quicker than the previous episode. I'd turn to music, books, the garden, the ocean, and friendships for fleeting moments of joy to carry me forward. For me, joy is the absence of pain. Joy is an innocent emotion and cannot be forced or fabricated. That is why I picked joy for my daily goal.

૭

My best friends are married couples who found it difficult to be with me after my husband died. It was a painful realization that I had to make a whole new social life.

~Gale P.

૭

I see people but I don't connect. I learned living alone that we live in a selfish world. People are insensitive. Many people hurt and others don't realize it or if they do, they don't care. The result is the same. I stay away from people in self defense. Other widows can be very cruel. I went to dinner with a few and one woman said, "It's been five years and you still see a therapist?" She still has her husband's clothes. I think that's sick. I now take one day at a time. I have lunch with one girlfriend and I share my feelings with my therapist.

~Nikki H.

૭

What really was an eye opener for me was that most of the people that we knew took off like bullets! They still do, including the person we trusted most—the executor of our estate. Can you believe that! At first, it hurt a lot. Now, I take it in stride. Nothing much hurts anymore. After all, when you have climbed Mount Everest, every other mountain seems like child's play. Oh yes, it makes you a little more cynical about the world. There are some exceptions but they are few and far between.

~Rhonda R.

ی

It's been a year since my husband died. I'm trying to make as many new friends as possible. It has tailored down since my husband died because I'm not in the mood to really engage in conversation. My friends have commented that I am less cheerful than before.

I have three groups of friends. There are singles, married without kids, and married with kids. I rarely go out with singles. My married friends have not avoided me. It's mainly the selected married with kids I feel most comfortable. I find some people to be touchy so I back away after the first outing.

My married friends without kids are very sensitive. The girls will go out without their spouses and I like this because it reminds me of the good old days when we went on our girly dates.

I rarely have the luxury to go out alone. Even if I had the time, it would probably be to church or to the hairdresser. However, when I am alone, I enjoy watching the body chemistry of couples. It's these times that I think about my husband and how we would have behaved. I realize that I took our body chemistry for granted. I wish I could turn back the clock.

~Allie P.

ی

I enjoy meeting new people. It seems easier at times to visit with someone that doesn't know that I am grieving. I feel stronger when I can learn new things and talk about new subjects.

~Sofia B.

Pronouns as a single really gives me problems. I've heard other widows and widowers use the "we" and "our" pronouns and wondered why. And now I struggle with this. I still use the "we" and "our," and I find I don't want to change to "me" and "mine." It makes my husband's death so final, which it is. Of course they will always be "our children" but I also think that it is "our farm" and "our house."

~Patti S.

I think sometimes that I'll never love again. I made it through the first year. It went by so quickly. Where did it go? I find it hard to even remember what took place during that time. I had finally found my soulmate. After a young, first marriage that ended in divorce, 10 years of dating and raising two children alone, I found the love of my life! Seventeen years. We held each other, kissed, and told each other every day how lucky we were and how much in love we were. We did everything together. We missed each other throughout the day and called just to say, "Watcha doin'?" I'm sitting here two years later and suddenly have an overwhelming feeling. I feel like I'm losing my mind. I have friends and family who love me but right this minute I feel so alone. I know it's time to join the world again but even the thought of someone else makes me cringe. I can't even look at another man without thinking of my husband and how I would betray him with thoughts of another. I float through the days praying, thinking and hoping for companionship. Hoping that my days will be filled again but always thinking that if I married again, he would just die and I could not go through that, not another time. I see people so in love, so happy. Just like I was. I miss that so much.

~Donna H.

ॐ

When I am really tied down with my daughter, I think about those couples who can do this completely without worrying they are losing their friends simply because they've got each other. Now, it's a challenge for me to juggle between my child and making new friends.

~Brady H.

ॐ

I seem to have lost my identity and because of this, I am groping in the dark. I find myself doing a lot of things differently from when my husband was around, although I am still doing things that he liked. I have stopped taking care of my face and skin, which seems an irony. I did all that when he was around.

~Brenda H.

ॐ

I was married and a happy housewife who could safely "flirt" with all the men because I was secure in marriage. Now two and a half years later, I am free to flirt. I have tried it and I can't do it. I'm not sure that I want to but I would like to. I have many wonderful women with whom I can really share and get close to. However, it is more difficult to form friendships with men without giving the wrong signals.

~Shelby J.

I'm really single. As I am moving into the second year, I cannot keep thinking that it's going to be harder for me. Reality is further sinking into me that my husband is never going to return. It's like his death within a year is easy to handle because you tell yourself that he has gone overseas like most people. However, in the second year, it's almost impossible to believe that a person who has gone away for so long is ever coming back.

~Angelina T.

I do seem to have a lot of women helping me. I think that generally people have an urge to help and feel that they are helping. I also have a feeling that mothers can relate so well to how my wife must have felt telling her children that she was going to die. And maybe they feel better helping me parent.

~Stanley T.

Planning a trip alone is difficult even if I'm visiting out-of-town family. I miss the fun of sharing the planning. I find it difficult making all of the reservations and the necessities to pack. I travel because life goes on.

~Jules H.

Each time I look at my wedding and traveling pictures I scrutinize every inch of my husband. I look at the way he held me and posed with me and it brings tears to my eyes. It is times like this where I tell myself he is the only one for me and I am going to reunite with him when my time is up.

I wish that he were still around to travel with me. We had so many dreams for our daughter. We were going to take her to Florida to see Disneyland. I'll have to do that alone now.

~JoAnn T.

These past few days, I have been feeling lousy physically and emotionally. I stood blankly at our vacation photos by the hallway, just thinking of the good times we had. I think we truly were a couple when we traveled, with no worries of work at all. We just let loose!

~Jacqui L.

Part IV

Coping with the Legal
Part of Life

The Money

*Y*ou were the Numbers Guy. When I met you, you said you were an accountant. I didn't know there were different types of accountants and I really didn't care. When we decided to get married, I just wanted to be in love. And as a bonus, I was so excited that I would never have to balance a checkbook again. I took algebra three times. Math was so difficult for me and word problems were impossible. Every three months I just traded checkbooks so they would balance themselves out. You thought I was adorable and funny but this system certainly wasn't going to work for you. I agreed and tried to dump it in your lap.

You disagreed. You said that I had to learn not to fear numbers. I had to know what things cost. I had to be responsible. I said, "Oh, but you are the Numbers Guy. I trust you. You can do it all." You disagreed. You had another idea, which we implemented. I had to write all of the bills so that I would be aware of what we made and what we spent. For your part, you would do all the bookkeeping and once a month you would present me with a spreadsheet that I was forced to read while you explained.

During the first year of explanations, I got nervous and when I saw categories like life insurance and anything that meant you could die, I got violently sick to my stomach.

One day, during our second year of marriage, you walked in with a three-ring notebook that was divided into financial sections. Your boss at work had given these notebooks out to everyone. The purpose was to organize your finances for your family. You eagerly took the book to your desk and started filling out all of information. You called it, "The Brown Book." I remember you writing down names of people to contact, locations of documents like the deed to the house, investments, and all of our taxes were lined up according to the years. I hated that book. I thought it was depressing. I never once sat with you as you updated it and I left it on the shelf as if it was invisible. You were going to live forever. It didn't really matter.

Steve had been a partner in a "big eight" accounting firm. Little by little, Steve taught me the mechanics of his job. It took over a year to learn. He took me in stages, always making sure that I comprehended what he described. The how-to of business enchanted me. He taught me basic accounting principles at a time I hated balancing a checkbook. He was brilliant at what he did. He managed our finances while we were married and when he got sick, I panicked. I remember breaking down into tears at the kitchen table, telling him that I couldn't handle my finances alone. This was a horrible moment. We had never acknowledged out loud that Steve could or would die. If I brought it up, would he think that I thought he was dying and lose hope? If I brought it up, was I self centered and selfish? But Steve was my best friend. He was my everything. He was the only person that I could talk to about this. So I trusted in my pile of tears and told him that I was scared to death to not only lose him but to be stuck with finances without him guiding me.

Steve looked at me from across the table and took my hand. He got up and put his hand on my shoulder. Then he took my hand again and said, "Follow me. It'll be okay." We walked into our home office and Steve took the brown book, which had been sitting there unopened by me for 12 years and placed it on the table. He turned on the computer and said, "I'm going to write you a letter and tell you exactly what to do. If anything ever happens to me, just follow the letter and don't do anything else. You will be fine. I promise."

He immediately wrote me a letter, essentially outlining what I'd need to do, how to do it, and whom to trust if he died. Then he made appointments and took me to meet the people—the lawyers and accountants—that I could learn to trust.

When Steve died, I went back to my old system that was primitive and unscientific. I acquired his bookkeeping but did it by hand in a three-ring notebook instead of using Quicken on the computer. I don't balance checkbooks. Ever. But I do have a new concept of money and of its comings and goings.

This was all a new thing for me. I was forced to learn, forced to face truths...and most of all, I was forced to find trust. I didn't want to, but I had to find trust in the old demons that lurked in my mind's skewed perspective of money matters. And I came to learn so much—about credit cards, wills, trusts and beneficiaries; about bookkeeping systems and bank accounts, investments, property taxes and retirement; about bills and insurance; about every dime and nickel and emotion that gets wrapped around a person.

I came to learn about power of attorney.

I came to be prepared for any legal hassle.

I came to understand all those scary things about money, so that I could take charge of my life.

I learned that the first year of widowhood is a unique

hell and it's best not to make any major decisions. Just get through each day the best you can. Things are different the second year.

I learned that some people can turn on you financially, even someone in your inner circle. It's best not to make life-changing decisions without the opinion of someone who is independent from your feelings.

I learned that I needed 10-plus death certificates because things popped up that I never expected.

I learned that it's vitally important to have a credit card with your own name on it before you lose your husband's credit history at his death.

I learned that it's possible that your husband can take his name off the cards before he dies to make it easier for you later on.

I learned that if you tell the people at the other end of the phone that you are newly widowed, although you ended up crying most of the time, people are so compassionate and kind. They want you to make it.

I learned that group health insurance provided by my husband's company automatically expired at 18 months and I needed to apply for my own policy.

I learned that it's okay to ask my accountant and lawyer numerous questions over and over again because I must understand. I learned to hire and fire until I made a team that felt like a family. I called all of these people, "Rent-a-husband."

I learned that no matter how emotional I got, I had to make good decisions to protect my future. I made the "48 hour rule." I couldn't make a big decision for 48 hours. I had to let emotions run their course.

I was a widow. I learned that there were people who would take advantage of my new stage in life but there were also people who were really there for me.

Life was becoming vastly different. It wasn't clear. It made no sense sometimes. I was in survival mode. That's all I knew.

I must admit that I get very frightened at times. What do I now put on those documents that say, "Who shall we contact in case of an emergency?" What if something happens to me at night? How will I be able to get help? Suppose I get really sick like he did? Will I have someone to come and stay with me eight to 10 hours a day? So many changes. So many things to think about. How will I go on with my life now? I don't sleep well at night and so I don't wake until nine or 10 AM. Sometimes I think, "What am I getting up for anyway?"

~Katrina K.

I did my part concerning the finances after my husband died. I passed the follow-up details to my cousin, a lawyer. Thankfully, my husband was a very organized and neat person who kept his things in order so retrieving these documents weren't a pain in my already painful spirit. In my country, we have to clear these matters in six month's time or else the government will charge us interest for estate duty. I think that I have done this part well because of my nature. I am a person who hates to sit on things, especially for urgent matters so I would prefer to settle them fast and get it out of the way. There was so much to do for my husband, despite his young age but because of the nature of his death, which was a car crash, I faced some difficulties, especially when getting the new car.

~Merna L.

Getting a new home never occurred to me until a church counselor brought it up. That was when I seriously looked at my finances and decided to look for a suitable place near my parents. I did house-hunting from late last year. Throughout that period, I was nursing a very sore and broken heart. I couldn't have imagined myself going through this on my own. The worse part of it all is not having someone close to you say, "This is the way to go. I think we are on the right track." It's all about making every decision, all on your own.

~Yvonne S.

It's painful to see documents on which your husband's name is no longer there. It's now your name or your dad's name. You start to ask yourself at times, "Why me?" This can't be true. But you just bounce back after this thought that flashes across your mind.

~Eleanor M.

I lost my dear husband to cancer. He was 54 and I am 52 this year. I can't stay at the house. I stay with my children. I can't make enough money to make it on my own. I am going to lose my home. I just found out I owe the IRS money from three years ago. It feels like I am on the planet with millions of people moving about and yet I am all alone. I don't know what I want to do. I don't have time to mourn. I have time to just keep trying to make a dollar.

~Katie M.

I learned something the hard way. I wasn't legally married to my love but we lived together for 15 years as husband and wife. We shared a home filled with our mementos and things we both brought to our relationship. Now I am told by the estate for his children that everything in this house now belongs to them. My love and I trusted that the heirs would be fair. Litigation is complicated in the United States because of no common-law status. I have to bring some sort of proof that we were indeed co-habituating. We did not file tax returns together as I had a separate corporation for my "estate planning." He went back and forth on how to do it and 15 years later, we didn't finish it. What is it said about the milk and not having to buy the cow? The time sneaks up and you forget about the long-term consequences. This is a miserable time and I am trying to work through it. Maybe I don't know what doors God will open.

~Cindy S.

Taxes, investments and savings, fortunately, were not a problem for me. I was the bookkeeper for the farming business. A farm accountant does the tax work for us. For years I have enjoyed the challenge of investing and feel comfortable handling the insurance money with the help of a close friend that opened an investment office in town just five years ago.

~Martina M.

My lawyer told me I have one final step to go before I am awarded the legal documents. These documents allow me to close all of my husband's accounts and obtain the final insurance payout. I am glad. It has taken one and a half years. At last!

~Mila Y.

A year and a half after my husband died, I moved to my new apartment and I suddenly felt a sense of completeness. I didn't feel a need to get material items to fill the void in my heart. I didn't visit the malls like I did after my husband died. But after a month in my new home, I seemed to have reverted to my old self. I have sort of concluded that I am buying things to fill a void in my heart, not because I genuinely need them. Perhaps, it's finding a new identity for myself. My preferences are fairly similar before and after my husband's death but now I feel I am buying to make myself happy, which is only temporary and I know it won't work. I guess as long as I am within my budget and spend what I can afford to pay, I should be fine.

~Erika B.

Part V

※

Growing Into Singlehood

Home Improvement

*W*e had relocated to our new home with big dreams for our future. This would be our dream house where we would retire. We had been in our dream home for 15 months when you got sick. The house was no longer a focus. The kitchen became a pharmacy; the den that only had two outdoor chaise lounges became a hospital room. We didn't have a couch.

When you died in the den and were no longer physically here, our home became impersonal to me. I left the house unfurnished and untouched for about two years. There was no point in buying something that you wouldn't be a part of. I rarely had anyone visit except a few very close friends. I had my bed to lay on and I sat at your computer. I stood when I ate at the counter so what was the point?

Surprise. One day I woke up and the grief had changed in my body. It changed on its own and I could feel the change of energy within me. A few days later, a friend had brought me a large poinsettia plant for Christmas. She brought it in and placed it in the entry. She said, "You need this plant. Your house is dead and it's been dead for too long." After she left, I walked around the house and decided that I wanted a home that had life in it. I didn't have a clue who I was, what I liked or what I wanted. I called the mother *of a student of mine who was a decorator. We made a plan and she helped me decorate.*

I find comfort in my house. It's alive and it's a real home to me now. I've found my own taste. I decorated the master bedroom in a very feminine style with feminine colors. I bought plants and put in speakers for music. I continue to grow and learn what I like. I'm not afraid to make mistakes. I make home improvements easily now. I love to walk through the garden and the house and see the things from my past. I have, however, removed a lot of memory filled knick knacks and pictures. I enjoy making new memories and bringing them inside my home. The joy I feel now is the feeling of warmth and balance inside my soul. I know Steve would be so proud to see who I've grown to be.

When my husband was still with me, we used to talk about redoing our bathroom. In our travels, I had discovered the Bidet. We had checked out the possibility of putting one in. I wanted one so badly but it meant a complete construction job. My husband felt he couldn't go through with it and would always joke, "You can do it over my dead body." Since he already had cancer, it was funny but not so funny. However, he had a way of making comments that were really humorous and kept things light under the circumstances. A year and a half after he was gone, I decided it was time to change things in the house. I had to let go of the past so I could move forward. After much thought and soul searching, I decided to redo the whole house and make it mine. I installed the new bathroom with the Bidet and updated the colors. I got rid of many things and gave the house a new feeling. I kept some of the things he purchased in our travels so he is represented but it is my house. I love the changes I have made. It has helped me to become the new single person I have to be in order to survive in this new life. I know that he is watching and smiling because I took his advice.

~Jolene S.

After my husband died, I had no desire to do anything. As time went on, I started burying myself in work and my son's activities to keep my mind very busy. There was a part of me that wanted to keep the house exactly as it was. However, I did decide to make changes to the house because I have always enjoyed decorating and remodeling our home. Making changes gave me the opportunity to think about what I wanted to do and kept me focused on happy things. However, I must admit, that when I made changes to my basement, everything in this area of the house was very sentimental to me. My husband received multiple awards posthumously. I have them all framed or encased. I have also displayed those items that were most important to him—pictures of his family and many fire department photos. Some people find the need to clear their home of items like clothing that remind them of their loved one. However, for me, I cannot bear to remove these things. These items hold very special memories for me and I have a strong need to preserve those memories.

~Tamara M.

After one and a half years of not listening to music, I have finally started to listen to music again. It started with the redecorating of my home. We had old speakers that stood on the floor. I had ceiling speakers installed in every room. The sound is fantastic. Redecorating was so exciting and it opened up a new world. Listening to music with these great speakers gives me such joy. I still don't listen to his favorite music but I have started getting new artists that I have discovered in recent months.

~Pam P.

My husband was brilliant at working around the house. If something broke, it was repaired immediately. I found myself asking every man I met for help in some way. I soon learned that there are some men who can never do anything and it was pointless asking them. Things that were so easy for my husband were not so easy for others. In my husband, I had an engineer, electrician, plumber, handyman, and car mechanic. You name it and he could fix it! His garage was equipped with all kinds of tools, lathes and nails for everything. He even fixed Barbie dolls, putting on a head or leg that came off. The children were delighted. Daddy could fix anything. I can ask two or three men about the same problem and they all come up with different solutions. And then what do I do? My decision making, never the best at anytime, posed enormous problems for me. I found it really difficult to make any changes.

~Emily M.

I felt that I was betraying my husband by letting his favorite car go. He loved that car and had taken great care of it and my car for the previous 10 years. After asking everyone I met for their opinion, I changed to the car of my dreams. It turned out to be a costly change, high insurance and the miles per gallon were so low that my weekly costs soared.

The following week after changing my car, the police arrived at my door to ask if I owned a white Ford Sierra Sapphire. It had been seen being driven recklessly by youths in another part of town. This hurt so much to know that his beautiful car was being abused this way. I could have kept it another six months and saved myself a lot of money.

~Robyn B.

〰

I'm experiencing day-to-day annoyances such as a faucet not working or the weather turning bad and the car not functioning. Always before, I could rely on my husband to "fix it." Now I find I have resources or rely on friends or neighbors, which hurts my pride. I have a lot of girlfriends but I sure miss the companionship of my husband.

~Ruth M.

〰

I can't stand the weekends and try to keep myself busy however I can. My husband always took care of the bills and the outside chores and now I am doing them. During his long illness, a lot of things fell by the wayside. But after his death, it kept me busy straightening things out.

~Renee S.

〰

It's been over a year and I still find myself adjusting to this role. Decisions have to be made alone. I have no one to speak to. I think that's the hardest part of grief. It's returning to an empty home, with just your daughter, and not having anyone to affirm your actions. It can be mentally depressing because we are humans after all. I have been learning it the hard way. I see my role as a challenge to better myself. I am now a driver, maid, breadwinner, electrician, financier, etc. Whatever I do, I have to consider doing it from my perspective, although I take advice from people now and then. But nothing beats having your spouse telling you to go ahead, this is the right decision.

~Ginny W.

Being naturally an independent, self-sufficient woman, I never thought of asking people for help. Never! It was only when I lost my husband that it was impressed upon me the importance of a good support system. I was in denial that this can't be. I shouldn't be asking people for help. You might call me arrogant. My husband's death was a humbling experience for me. If anything isn't right, I have learned to immediately ask for help.

~Dana G.

Dating Again

$\mathcal{I}$ remember our last conversation before you died as if it were yesterday. You said to me, "You are the most wonderful wife, friend, and partner a man could ever want. Every dream I ever had came true because of you. The only dream I won't get is growing old with you. You are so young and so full of life. I want you to fall in love again and have another relationship."

"I want to go with you," I pleaded. "I wish it were me and not you. I don't want to be left here without you."

"You still have work to do here. You need to work with the kids and help them. Your work is not done. And when it is, and it's your turn, I will come back and cross you over," he said as if he knew this would be the case.

I heard what you said but it made no sense to me. You, as always, were so supportive and loving. You had promised to take care of me when you married me and you were trying to take care of me as you were leaving me. It was just too much. You gave me your blessing to move on and be happy. You seemed to be able to read the future and know exactly what I needed. The future was impossible because it was dying with you.

After you died, I went to the beach three or four times a week and sat on a bench, silently staring at the water with *tears rolling down my face. For weeks, I silently shared the bench with a man a little younger who happened to show up at the same time. We eventually spoke minimum words about the waves, birds and sunsets. One day, he introduced himself. His name was Steve. Your name. I shook his hand and walked away. I didn't return. Hearing your name was just too much.*

I decided from then on that I would walk along the water's edge. After a few weeks, a man about my age stopped me and introduced himself. It seemed we lived in the same neighborhood but I never noticed him. He couldn't believe it. We actually passed each other walking on the street. The truth was, I saw no one. I was drowning in grief. I didn't explain myself.

As it turned out, our schedules were the same and for months we would meet up on the sand to walk and watch sunsets. I enjoyed his stories and listened intently, speaking only about him. One evening, he asked me to dinner. I replied, "No, I can't take you off the sand." He thought I was shy. I wasn't. We walked to the parking lot together. For the first time, he hugged me goodbye. I froze like ice. I turned and walked away without speaking.

Dating was something I learned to do over four years. I took dancing and singing lessons to get in touch with myself. I had a lot of counseling to try and get in touch with my feelings and to help me to re-enter the world. The dating world was something I knew that I had to enter if I didn't want to be alone forever. I needed single friends now. I joined a women's group and participated in the "It's Just Lunch" dating service. Solitude wasn't good for me. I needed to get out. I had no agenda to love again or to be loved. My goal

was to find joy being busy.

I was a new person now. The grief and loss of my husband had changed me forever. I couldn't replace my old life. I needed a new one. Everyone in my world believed I would find love again. They felt I would find a companion, someone I enjoyed hanging out with. No one really thought I could love deeply again but at least I would have company that I enjoyed. I couldn't see it but it was great to have them believe for me when I couldn't.

There she was, a blonde goddess with nothing on but a big smile, exposing her womanhood in front of my face. Whereas I would not have been caught dead to be seen in a "Gentlemen's Club" earlier that year, my life had changed and there I was at the invitation of some professional colleagues. Nothing aroused me. I was emotionally numb.

I lost my wife to medical complications and pneumonia after an elective operation near our 25th wedding anniversary seven years ago. Not even her doctor anticipated her demise. She had experienced more than her fair share of medical maladies in her lifetime and she was finally at peace and out of pain. It took some considerable professional therapy for me to later understand why I could not produce a tear during her passing. I hadn't cried since I was nine years old. By the time my daughter graduated, I could cry again. It took me several months to deal with the fact that I was a widower and single. It took all the effort I had to crawl out of bed each work day and come out of seclusion on the weekends. I pretended that her closet did not exist.

It took several months before I ventured out in public without wearing the ring I had worn daily for 25 years. Although I had the courage to take this first step as a single person, my self-esteem was so low that I had absolutely no expectation of being attractive to women again. There was a time near that of my nude dancer experience that I contacted an escort service for the only purpose of having dinner with a woman. I felt that I looked unattractive. I projected that feeling and discounted any sign of attraction from women. I believed that I would go to my grave a single man void of any form of intimate female companionship.

I finally mustered up the courage to ask a Meg Ryan look-alike to dance at a lounge that I frequented. We danced until closing time and she gave me her number. I was absolutely smitten. She sparked the beginning of a journey of bachelorhood experiences beyond my wildest dreams. That feeling of having my first boyhood "crush" again overwhelmed me. I started to behave more confidently around women. I started to notice occasional glances and deliberate conversations while shopping. My persona was becoming more open and receptive. It was not long before, as an active and available bachelor, I was "out there."

"Which one was that?" my daughter asked me after hanging up the phone in my kitchen six years later. I responded that she was a new dating interest, which was probably the third I had that month. My son and daughter had witnessed me going from emotional numbness to a kid in a candy store on the dating scene. They had met most of them and only approving of a few. They were either "nuts" or "after my money." They were mostly blonde and my kids were right. My seven years of bachelorhood led from emotional numbness and lack of self confidence to arranging to satisfy four women in three days in Las Vegas. I had the good fortune of traveling extensively with an out of town "friend with benefits" while keeping company with a number of attractive, and yes, blonde goddesses near home. I had become a skilled "player." I was enjoying my bachelorhood. A few of the relationships were also exclusive and serious. "Playing" can get to be tiring and marginally rewarding. I was becoming "played" out. I was at such a fine state of self-awareness and self-confidence that I began telling women not to waste my time unless they were available for a committed relationship. I was done playing around. I had sampled enough and was ready to select my entrée.

I am now happily married to someone who was preparing for me while I was in preparation for her. We are like the tumblers in a slot machine that drop at the right time to produce a jackpot. My theory on life relationship development came to me while touring a motorcycle exhibit in Las Vegas is as follows:

We come in to this planet with a full set of "teeth on our sprocket." They might be baby teeth. We might lose a few over time. Depending on how many teeth on our sprocket we have at any one time, we can only rotate that sprocket so fast. When we grow, or grow out of, relationships, we find ourselves peddling at different speeds and not traveling together. When one loses a life partner, it is like having one's emotional gears stripped. It takes effort and getting back on the bike by being out there in the single scene to begin to grow those teeth back. That explains the transitional relationship and even the playing when you enjoy breaking your own speed records. When you finally know your own riding potential and can recognize that of another person, you can consider having another life relationship. Someone once asked me why I did not pursue such a relationship with a female best friend. At that time, my best answer was that she was not a blonde. In reality, I was still growing teeth while she was growing some herself. The powers of this universe do not make mistakes. They provide opportunities for those who are ready for them. We became ready at different times and the universe provided us loving people worthy of the commitment and joy we experienced before having our gears stripped. There is hope. There is opportunity.

~Edward H.

Nothing makes sense. I'm dating someone I like very much. And yet, it's been almost two years since my wife died and a day doesn't go by that I don't think about her. It's always the little things. It's a song on the radio, a phone call, a smell or a movie.

~Dave O.

I did think I was ready for a proper relationship. We had talked about moving on and I am sure I did much of my grieving when my wife was unwell. However, in the developing relationship I had recently (now over), I found that it was harder than I thought to let anyone fully into my life. Perhaps it would be different with someone else, someone I did think was very special. Anyway, it has been a positive thing and I am not averse to having other dates. I will just take it easy and one day at a time.

~Ben P.

My darling wife died almost seven years ago from cancer. She was in the hospital for three weeks and home for four weeks. When she died, I felt so alone, so angry. I still do at times. When I go out with people, I find myself comparing them with her. I know that's not fair of me but I can't help it. My friends up North call and wonder why I haven't gotten married. They just don't understand. It's not like your car dies and you go out and get another one. It's not that simple. Only if you have lost someone you love and lived with for so long can you even begin to understand how it feels.

~Jimmy M.

I had my first dinner date this week. It was a blind date, my first and last!! Ha! It was a step and I feel better having taken it but I would feel better with a more conventional situation.

~Paul J.

I have a new relationship but it comes with an awareness. It can end. Period. The reason doesn't matter. It can end. I will never really be safe with someone in the forever way. There is no forever. Men leave. They divorce or die. I never really knew that. But I have me and I have to always work on me. I must take one day at a time and just do my best. I must stay in the moment.

~Lolli G.

I have a new boyfriend. I am happy with him but he questions if I have let go of my first love enough to fall in love with him. What can I do? I can't ever completely let go of my first love but do I put away the pictures to move on? I have all these unanswered questions about dating now and I don't know what to do with them. They are all questions I must figure out on my own. I just wish I knew all of the answers without going through the pain and without making mistakes. I am feeling very happy with my boyfriend but it is a scary feeling and I don't want to mess up the good things I have now by pushing him away or not letting him in completely. I am also scared because I feel that nothing good stays in my life. I feel when things are going good, something will always come crashing down. It's been almost 16 months since he died and I am not sure what to do with my sadness.

~Candace B.

Transitional Man

It's been two years since you died. I have known this man for a while on a casual basis. We talk freely on the rare occasions that we meet. He is so comfortable for me. I like his heart. My heart is dead. We have nothing in common and come from different worlds. He is patient and he knows that this is a moment in time. I am about to have a transitional relationship, not an affair, not a long-term relationship.

The first time he hugged me I began to feel again. The ice was melting. The first time he kissed me the ice melted completely. I was feeling again. I had missed the human touch. He was so gentle, caring, strong and loving. The physical release that I thought was dead opened the wound in my broken heart and I howled for the first time since the day I saw Steve dead.

I sobbed hysterically for the physical and emotional pain my husband had gone through. I sobbed for the pain I had for losing him and helplessly watching him die. I sobbed for his arms missing around me and his thoughts and words. I missed his arms at that moment more than ever. I finally let it all out. This transitional man held me close and said over and over, "It's okay. You're okay. I'm not going anywhere."

My transitional man stayed in my life for six months as I transitioned from death in my soul to life again. He was a moment in time. I was so grateful for this part of my new beginning. I could not have done this part alone. I needed the human touch.

The comment my brother-in-law made to my kids when he met my first girlfriend after my wife's death was "you usually start with the low hangin' fruit when you're pickin' a tree." My kids were kind enough to keep that to themselves for a while, but it did cause me to think about why I fell for a redhead eight years my senior when I was later dating arm-candy Newport Beach blonde babeage.

George Clooney might have summed it up in the movie *Oh, Brother Where Art Thou* when he said: "It is a fool who seeks wisdom in the chambers of the heart." Neuroscientists would support the notion that our brain—instead of the heart—plays a big part in our emotional behavior. Peptides are released when certain connections are made in the brain that causes us to want contact with certain types of individuals, substances, activities and so forth. So what caused my peptides to come alive again with my particular transitional relationship? There was something beyond the outer features of that person that caused my neurons to spring to life.

When we experience the loss of a loved one, particularly a spouse, we typically grieve and go through a depression that has us feeling doubtful that another such relationship could ever again exist. The peptides shut down in that department, so to speak, and Emotional Alzheimer's or Cerebral Sclerosis sets in. Eventually a person steps into our life when we are more ready to be a receptor to another's peptide reactions. A warm hug and prolonged eye contact did it for me. When Ms. Transition looked up at me for the first time, our eyes locked and we began looking further into each other's spirit as time went on.

We began dating and spent countless hours on the phone as this was also a long distance relationship. She had divorced her husband about a year prior to us meeting and currently had an abusive boyfriend who she was in the process of leaving.

She attended group meetings for people with co-dependant tendencies, which I qualified to join at my stage of emotional awareness at that time. It was a perfect match for our neuroses. I was particularly neurotic about concealing the budding relationship from my children. After all, their late mother was young and pretty. Ms. Transition had seen better days. There was also the issue of betraying the memory of their late mother. Nonetheless, I was in the deep end of the pool before long with great sex and emotional comfort.

It ultimately came time to bring Ms. Transition out of the closet. The introduction to my teen-age daughter was a disaster to say the least. Talk about being cruel; I walked right in to a spinning buzzsaw. However, that experience did send a clear signal to my daughter that Dad was ready to see women and she began focusing some positive energy towards me by giving me feedback about my choices.

As my ego and self confidence restored themselves, so was my growing awareness of attractive women. My swimming skills were improving thanks to the time spent with Ms. Transition in the deep end of the pool. Had it not been for her, I would have not gone on to date several other women that my daughter could not stand, yet ultimately find one that she has grown to trust and respect: my wife.

Oddly enough, Ms. Transition was probably the most fun and level headed woman I dated outside of my wife. Neither one of them was similar to any of the women I dated in between. I have also been Mr. Transitional to several of them and met their needs in the same light. Outside of one's ultimate life partner, I believe that the bond developed in the transitional relationship remains the strongest and can offer inner comfort that you will always be loved.

~Edward H.

I have a big church background. I have counseled others and now as a widow, I have first-hand experience on counseling widows. I know the rules about being widowed. Don't do anything serious for one year, especially dating, selling, moving. My husband had been sick for many years. So when he died, I thought that I had grieved during the years before. My kids had moved out and the "empty nest" had set in. I looked to the world that I was doing just fine. My concerned friends said that I was "far" more "together" than most. The point is, I chose to push a relationship with a man that I had known for years believing that the sooner I could be that "Housewife" role again and kick back into a more familiar lifestyle, the better life would be. I never realized how messed up I was from the trauma of being the caregiver and losing the man I was going to grow old with and rock our grandbabies with together. So, with that, I married this man that I knew, a friend, one year and one week after my husband died.

It was so unhealthy from the start. We were together for 10 months and I told my new husband that I just couldn't do it anymore. I had been pretending that the last 26 years never happened. I had never considered if we were both emotionally and physically healthy. Yes, another huge mistake. Right before we got married, we found out my new fiancée had a disease that would get worse as time went on. I was losing ground and we separated trying to give me some time, which only slowed the grieving down even more. I filed for a divorce last September and it went through last month. What I say is this. When people say wait one year before making any heavy decisions, this should include not even starting a new relationship until a year is over. However, I have seen it work, especially when some of my male friend widowers get married soon after their loss so I do realize that there are some success stories. It's so individual but in most cases, I believe that it is still taking a huge risk.

I am sharing all of this to try to convey that three years later, I find myself having a second chance to learn how to embrace the pain. Lord willing, I will get some healing on how to go on alone when our lives and dreams have been shattered into a million pieces. I feel it's all about the right timing and really following your heart as to whether that person is sent as a gift from God and is it His timing. I look back and now see so clearly all of the red flags, the lack of peace, and how I didn't follow my heart because I was trying to avoid the deepest pain I pray I will never have to go through again.

~Roberta P.

The Future

My mother kept encouraging me to never turn down an invitation. She promoted joining groups, doing what I love and to keep dating when the opportunity would arise. It wasn't that I was afraid to let anyone in again, romantically or not. I met people and made friends with men who could have been potential romantic interests but it took me years to get into the dating groove again and truly be interested in the person. I was bored with the lunch dates after one hour. That was enough for me. You are a hard act to follow.

I wanted company but I couldn't get passed the boredom. I was happier at the beach alone or listening to my music or just being with my friends. My heart was somewhere else, always with you. I couldn't receive and I couldn't give. I kept going because my mother said, "Practice. Practice getting dressed and having conversation. Someday, it will become second nature again." I kept trying. I was 50 years old and I needed my mother's wisdom. You've been gone a very long time.

I had gotten comfortable with my baby steps and a handful of people in my inner circle told me to join the Internet to meet new people. They had done it successfully or had friends that had really enjoyed their experiences. I said no for a long time. Feeling very stuck one day, I asked for *help from my cousin and a girlfriend who were members of an Internet dating service to help me fill out an application. Another friend took my picture. I hesitantly joined.*

I never chose anyone to meet. I enjoyed the men selecting me and I enjoyed e-mail. I didn't have to talk. Only on a rare occasion would I speak to anyone. It was my "delete" game and it filled up my nights.

Two months after I joined, Mr. Right e-mailed me. His words, picture and profile grabbed me and I felt comfortable. This was odd. Actually a bit scary, but I had a good feeling. For the first time in four and a half years, I felt romantically vulnerable. We chatted online and then we chatted on the phone. Eventually we met. I knew in my heart that night he was special. He was the one. I believed and still do that you sent him to me.

Our relationship kept blossoming. I was entering a new chapter in my life. It was so easy to give. I was alive giving. I didn't know how hard receiving would be until a few months later at his house. He had surprised me by showing me a bathroom that he now considered mine. I put some items away and stood in the doorway.

I was moving forward. The toothbrush on the sink didn't mean I was replacing my husband. I was having a brand new life. Mr. Right saw me standing in the doorway crying. He came over and silently held me. Then he said, "This is big." I cried more and he held me tighter.

I didn't miss my husband's arms. Mr. Right's arms, integrity and character were strong and I wanted him and his arms around me. Knowing this, I cried even harder. The love I have for my husband hadn't left, it never will. It just went into a different part of my heart. I want and need to love this new man. I love being part of a couple again.

It's easy to love this man because I know how precious love and time are. I treasured every moment of the day with my husband. Now, with an awareness of how quickly it can all leave, I love this man daily like a precious treasure. I don't want to waste a minute of time with him. It doesn't mean that I'll forget my husband, ever. And my new man doesn't expect me to. Steve is in the cells of my body and sometimes in my dreams. I know his energy will always check in on me when I need him. But I'm okay now. It's a brand new me in a brand new life. I thank my husband daily for his words before he died encouraging me to fall in love, have another relationship and to be happy.

No one blames us if we change our minds about things we promised to people we love. We make promises when we were married. I made promises as a wife and now I'm a widow. Letting go is not the same thing as forgetting. It's not even close.

~Lois P.

Two and a half years ago, my husband died and left me alone. I didn't think life would be acceptable. It has been a struggle. After a while I made the decision to meet new people by doing activities I enjoyed like dancing classes and bridge. I even tried lawn bowling. I volunteered to usher at a theater. Now, I feel great! I have met and made new friends. I am living a single life and am comfortable with it. Being busy and feeling loved and cared about by my new friends and special family members, has made each day something to look forward to. My new friends have introduced me to new adventures and I never say no to invitations. Some are successful and some disappointing but it keeps me alive and moving forward. However, I miss my husband, my best friend. I still have a hole in my heart, which I know will never go away. The bottom line: I am feeling great physically now and I am better company so I get invitations to go to dinner. I am planning things for the future! I am looking forward to traveling, which is something I love. The secret I learned is time helps but we must help ourselves. It takes time to have the courage to step out and live again. Some days it seems hopeless but I keep moving.

~Kay L.

Today I was singing in my small church choir. My husband always sat to the left of me in the bass section. The anthem we sang needed his strong bass voice and yet it was not there. Another small and yet enormous section of my life was not there. How do I weep in the middle of an anthem? He is there with me and yet he is not there with me. The journey of grief moves on...alone...always alone.

~Helen R.

My husband died in his sleep in a fire three years ago. I survived but everything that I had known was violently taken away and is forever gone. I have made mostly new friends as some of the couples kind of drifted away from me and I let them. It's been hard, but I am seeing people (disappointed by my grown children) and life goes on.

~Laurel R.

I started dating a woman and my daughter withdrew from me. Finally, she opened up and said, "If I like your girlfriend, mom will know and be mad and jealous. Your girlfriend is so pretty with her long brown hair and she's a lawyer. Mom is so different."

I told my daughter that there would never be anyone who means as much to me as mom does. No one will ever take her place or her sister's place in my heart.

I explained that Mom would never be mad at any of us for liking someone new. When someone we love dies, we get sad but we must not hang on to that kind of sad for so long that it prevents us from loving others. Love is meant to be shared.

~Bruce H.

Last night was the first time in a long time that I cried myself to sleep. I was thinking about my boyfriend, my love, and our first date. We went on a date on a Friday and then we were together every day and night after that until he died. I way lying alone last night as my current boyfriend was in the living room watching TV and I just couldn't help thinking about my other relationship and reliving our first weekend together. I thought it was odd that I was thinking about our first date and when I woke up this morning, I realized that yesterday was the anniversary of our first date. I didn't consciously realize that last night but it must have been in the back of my mind yesterday. It has been almost two and a half years and I can't believe I am still hurting this much, especially when I am in love with my current boyfriend. It makes me feel as if I shouldn't even be in a relationship if I am missing my first love so much. It's also not something I feel I can open up to my boyfriend about because it would hurt his feelings. It's strange how our bodies are aware of certain dates and memories that come to the surface when we are least expecting it.

~Helene F.

We know the presence of our dearest on the other side, as it is felt in tingles on the back side. We love to the fullest those in our bedside. We love in the moment, forever, and always never denied.

But some things we know,

We know near and dear,

What might be vague to others,

We know very clear.

There are moments to be treasured,

That come un-expected,

When our hearts are heavenly touched and least un-protected.

Brief feelings of grief, sadness, sorrow and emotion.

To experience great sunsets, on a sun swept ocean.

To know my commitment to eternal devotion.

~Marshall H.

There are moments when I reflect and might not be as emotionally available to my life partner as I would otherwise be if I were not a widower but I make up for it by being more intensely available most of the time. I am never certain if my life partner understands my emotional travel as I ineffectively try to conceal it, but I know it is a good thing to be able to be touched by the "other side" and flow with the experience. Louis Armstrong was once asked the question, "What is jazz?" His response was, "If I have to explain it to you, you will never understand it." Being widowed is something we would never wish on anyone nor expect anyone else to understand having not experienced it. We are blessed, however, if we continue to bring those dearly departed into our emotions, experiences, and joys as they occur while we enjoy our time on this planet.

I had a near brush with mortality recently and know that I survived by the grace of love from those around me. My work in not finished and I was reminded to be around to do it.

~Daniel F.

One of my wife's friends told me today that someday I'd meet someone and have the love I had for my wife. My answer was, "No." You only have that love once. I may meet someone and love them but never like I loved my wife.

~Allan V.

People around me tell me that one of these days, I'll meet someone again. My answer is, "Hey! When is that day ever going to come!" I am sick and tired of listening to such nonsense because the day might never come if God chooses to take us home. At my husband's wake, people close to me and not close to me came up to me and told me to call them when I need help. Would I ever call someone if they weren't close to me? And how about the fact they didn't leave their numbers behind?

~Chandra Z.

I have met a beautiful man whom I love and adore. I have been blessed. He is tolerant and understanding. Without him, I don't know what state the kids and I would be in now. I am scared, though, that he won't wait forever. He may not wait for me to give him my full time and affection. His father married a young widow with children so maybe he knows I may never be whole and he will always share me with my angel.

~Joy O.

I just got back from a holiday visiting family in another country. The trip was fun and I think the kids and I bonded as family even more. There were a number of people who commented that the kids were great and amazing. The security guard at the airport told me that my kids were so good and that I was great with them. We spent a lot of quality time together and even the long airplane ride was "us" time. We were doing things and experiencing things together as a threesome. I started to think that when my wife first died, I felt I was left on my own with the kids. On this holiday, I felt like we were a "family" doing things together. I knew that I wasn't "left" looking after them. We were a real family of three and I feel good about this.

~Jacob S.

Part VI

❧

Realities of Raising Children Alone

The Children

*H*ow do you tell your daughter that according to the doctor's estimation, you have four months left to live? We can't even acknowledge this ourselves. We refuse to believe it. Her mother died when she was 10 and I became her stepmother when she was 12. What do we do?

You told me you wanted her to have only happy memories of the last time she saw you because at age 10, she had seen her mother dead and you didn't want a repeat. Since she was 22 years old and lived on the other side of the United States, this was easy. We flew her out and spent time visiting. You looked great and felt great. No one could tell the hell you were living. The only thing different was your lack of hair from chemo. She had a great time. That was her final, in person, memory. As a father, you controlled that well.

Two years after you died, Steve, she got married. My stepfather walked her down the isle. Her fiancé stood on one side of her and your picture stood proudly on a table next to her. As the minister spoke, she got hysterical crying. Everyone sat in silence. I hadn't yet met the new people in her life or her fiancé's relatives. I stood up and said to the audience, "She is okay. Her father passed away and she misses him very much today."

Two years later your daughter had a baby boy. They named him Steven, after you.

Steven is walking now. Alex, my Mr. Right, and I went to see him. My stepdaughter truly believes that Alex was sent to all of us by her father from Heaven. She watched Alex talking baby talk to Steven as he held the baby on his lap. They were a natural fit. She saw how we all interacted and she wanted Steven to call Alex, "Grandpa." We all know and acknowledge that no one can be replaced. The baby was named after his mother's father. Period. However, we have learned something very important. We can choose to make a family. Baby Steven deserves to have grandparents and an intact family and extended family. It's up to us to move forward and give it to him.

When the baby was an infant and I watched Alex bounce him on his knee and coo to him, I fell apart inside. I was so sad that Steve wasn't physically there to be a part of this. At the same time, I felt so fortunate that Alex was exactly the kind of man who was filled with an abundance of love, an open heart, and was able to embrace this family and help it begin with a new wholeness and new traditions. It was rough on my heart for the entire visit because I felt like I was in a tug of war with the past and the present. I kept my feelings to myself and tried to stay in the moment. It was a difficult visit for me.

It's easier now. Another year has gone by. Things are more familiar. Patterns are being established. Bondings are taking place within the family. Steven has a brother now. Our family is growing.

When I turn to my fellow grievers on the Internet, I feel their pain. As I am evolving and moving forward every day, I read their e-mails with compassion. Absorbing their grief and experiences brings me to tears. Some people are "stuck" in those early experiences. Others are working hard to move through those early stages. I don't believe time heals for what some refer to as closure but I do believe that with hope and understanding of the grief after journey, my fellow grievers will be able to find joy again differently. This type of grief can turn us into hopeless children and I am honored to be a part of their journey forward.

I've been thinking about how to bring up my kids without my wife. I would want to bring them up as she would, but I'm me. However, I have been thinking about my life with my wife. No one can live with someone like her for nearly 17 years and not learn and imbue thoughts and approaches to life. It is difficult separating the "me" from the "us." The kids will naturally have "us" bringing them up.

~Robert J.

My daughter went out on Friday night. I told her that her Mum would be proud. My daughter believes that her mother is looking down proudly and seeing her. I am getting upset thinking that if my wife came back, some things would be different. The kids have new clothes, there is a new fridge. The little one doesn't nap anymore. I'm moving on but I want my wife to recognize things. It really upsets me.

~Ryan D.

My mom got a new car a couple of days ago. She wanted my husband to see the car even though he was in Heaven. So my parents, my sister, my two-year-old daughter and I drove to the columbaruim where my husband is buried. My daughter announced that she was visiting her Papa. I teared instantly. When we went up to the niche, she kissed the niche and said, "Hi." She was holding a beanie cat. When my dad told her to pray to her father, she took the cat's arms and put them together.

~Lannie L.

∽

What is most painful to me is going to my daughter's classes and seeing fathers around. I try to brush this emotion aside. Thankfully, it's temporary.

~Phyllis M.

∽

That first year it was so difficult to do all of the things we had enjoyed the year before. Most difficult were all the things associated with school: the visits to school to discuss progress with the teacher; and sports day when he was always at the finishing line encouraging both daughters to run as fast as they could. For that first year, I found it very painful to visit the school and see the memories of my husband as a great father. Every time I went to the school, the tears tumbled down as I remembered the happy events. I often left the school crying, going home to a house that was empty and lonely without him.

~Beatriz M.

∽

Our children moved schools from a primary school to a grammar school. It was very emotional when the oldest left in June. Dad was there for the transition and we had so much fun through the previous seven years. It is the youngest one's turn to change schools in June. The transition will be a difficult one as we leave all those happy memories and move forward to the unknown.

~Grace H.

Homework was another area that dad excelled in. With his years in the Merchant Navy, his gift for telling stories from around the world, and his wealth of knowledge, he was better than any encyclopedia with answers for everything. He made sure that they knew their spelling and that homework was done before they left for school. That first year, the content and quality of their schoolwork deteriorated. It is only beginning to get better now after two years.

~Bonnie M.

Just before their dad died, our oldest daughter went to her new school. These first two years have been especially difficult for her. We miss Dad's discipline. He controlled discipline and I was the easy-going one. He fought my battles. I am finding it so difficult with a girl who was entering the teenage years when he left us. It has been especially difficult distinguishing between the grief and teenage rebellion.

~Toby L.

Raising a teenager has been really difficult and I often wish I could have something to read about the combination of grief and teenager years. I have cried more tears about this. Although I have been doing "well," this has been the most trying of my days alone. I have been to all the counseling organizations for individual help and family help, too. I have phoned all the help lines for support and prayer at all times of the day and night. These all had their place and were useful through the first one and a half to two years. Then I realized that help has to come as an inner source, from oneself. I have prayed and called out to God. Now I am practicing reflexology. Kinesiology has been helpful, too, for the girls and for me. Both of these therapies treat the whole person— physical, mind and spirit. I do feel better on the days when I can get out for walks and go swimming.

~Victoria P.

I seem to have a lot of women helping me. I never thought that would happen. There is actually a reasonable queue as well. I think that generally people have an urge to help and feel that they are helping. I also have a feeling that mothers can relate so well to how my wife must have felt telling her kids that she was going to die. Maybe they feel better helping from this parenting angle.

~Edwin W.

Raising kids alone worries me a bit. It really does fill me with a sense of challenge and also some sense of privilege. It makes me dog-tired. I'm finding that I obviously now have to do things I didn't do as much like clothes shopping, haircuts, arranging with other parents the kid's trips, etc. But the big thing that I find so hard is being the sole source of discipline, fun, food (the kids actually ate two dinners while holding their noses!), well, everything. I've always been a hands-on Dad, even more so since we started on the journey with their mother having cancer, but the toughest thing in all this is the "soul" bit. My wife and I, together, would always just about get it right and we'd talk things through afterwards. Now it's just me. I reflect a lot on the little things. Should I have let my daughter stay up an extra 10 minutes?

~Derek K.

～

My daughter is in her third week of childcare today. Looking back, we have gone through so much during this challenging time. I've also realized that settling her into childcare is a lot harder than my personal grief work. At least I can control how I want to perceive various grief issues with myself. But my preschool daughter can't tell me how she is feeling about childcare. I have to be sensitive to pick up her cues and learn along the way. It's frustrating as well when you don't have the answer and when you are all alone.

~Monica S.

～

Seeing her smile makes my day. I feel so much joy when she chuckles. When she cries, I feel the pain. Each day I drop her off to school, I feel lightened. Lightened as in, I've managed to get up and take ourselves out of bed, drive to school, give her milk, all within 40 minutes.

~Shira J.

～

I just went to my youngest son's wedding. Soon, I will be going to see my only daughter graduate at college. I am flooded by emotions with not having my husband by my side. I am very teary eyed. These are special occasions for me. I did have a friend, a nice gentleman, who was at my side at the wedding. He has escorted me to two other weddings. He is a very good dancer and I enjoy dancing. We are just friends. I still miss my husband terribly. I did enjoy the wedding but the hardest part was the picture taking. The bride's parents were by her side and I was all alone, next to my son. I felt so alone! The next day, I saw my daughter accept an award as I sat by myself in tears. I was once again experiencing something new, feeling like a single parent. However, that is exactly what I am. I made the best of it but felt anger and betrayed by my husband for not being there. I did feel his spirit and presence, though, at both the wedding and at the college. I know my daughter missed her daddy, too. I realize that there will be more firsts, such as these types of events and it is really rough.

~Sharon W.

The girls' grief is a complicated thing. I'm treading on egg shells. I want them so much to grieve and talk but I don't want to push. I so much, so much, want to do the right thing. I feel like a crap Dad. I feel like an ace Dad.

~Jarrett Z.

If I could have my wife back for maybe five minutes, I would want to share the little things. I have really no profound statement to make and no big issues to resolve. It's just that invariably, there are little things that make me so upset, like wanting her to see the new things in the house and the kids' new clothes.

~Daniel E.

Today was a better day concerning childcare. My daughter got out of the car at childcare and went into the arms of the teacher without tears. Yesterday, I took the opportunity to bring her to another school opposite my apartment to see happy mothers pick up happy kids. I explained to her that many children go to school just like her and her mommy will pick her up just like she did today. I wish I didn't have to do childcare. She is just too young.

~Rachel M.

There are many events that are for dads and their children. I get disturbed on these weekends. I think about my husband's absence. I am sitting there alone with my daughter. I tell myself to focus on her, this class is for her, after all. It's just 45 minutes. But I think about balancing her gym class on Saturdays with church on Sundays. I do the best that I can with God's help.

~Jillian H.

Last week, my daughter and I went to pick up my dad from the airport. I was quite visibly upset when I saw children and wives waiting in anticipation for the dad/husband to return. I was staring at their hugs and kisses and listening to their conversations like, "Hi, Dad! Glad to see you home." I wondered what my daughter was thinking. I wondered how she would react if her father walked off that plane. When she saw her grandfather at the carousel to claim his baggage, she was screaming with joy. That answered my question. I felt relieved to see her so happy to see her grandfather.

~Janis P.

My daughter is so young. Last night, we were playing with dough. I decided to sing the song, "I Am a Little Teapot." My daughter said, "You cannot sing that song. Only Uncle can sing with me. My daddy can sing this song." I asked her, "Who is your daddy?" My two year old replied, "It's Uncle." It broke my heart. I cried and took a tissue to wipe my tears. She, too, went out and came back cleaning her eyes. I asked her what she was doing. She replied, "I am sad, Mommy." And we continued to play.

~Shar L.

My daughter is beautiful and five years old. It's getting close to celebrating her next birthday followed by Christmas. She has not stopped talking. She has been my shadow. My daughter mentions her Mum every time I say goodnight. She says she loves me to death but she loves Mum more because she's dead. Then she says, "I miss Mum."

Tonight I left her after having said our goodnight as usual. I heard her crying. When I came back in, she was sobbing, which was very, very unlike her. My lovely girl said, "I want Mummy." She was crying properly now.

We hugged and I told her how much Mum loved her and how she thought she was special. I told her that I loved her so much (I was brushing away her tears and she was doing mine) and that I would always love her and be there for her.

"Even when I'm a woman?"

"Yes, even when you're a woman. And you won't want

me to be there trying to look after you then!" She told me she wanted her Mum again. She also asked me a few times recently if humans can be angels or fairies. She really wants to be one. She has also been asking a lot of questions about what it will be like when she has a baby and is a Mummy.

~Paul D.

If I reflect back to the day that my husband was killed, I am flooded with painful memories—one of the most painful of which was going to my son's elementary school to pick him up and deliver the news that his Dad was dead. The look on his face is forever burned in my mind. I remember that he would not eat that day or for several days to follow. I remember holding him in the bathroom as he was getting sick and making a promise to him that I would be the best mother that I could be. I assured him that we would get through this together. The truth is that I was scared. I knew I would be raising my son by myself in his most difficult years, his teenage years, and I did not know how my son would be impacted by my husband's/his father's murder. They were very close. My husband was an extremely involved father who spent lots of time with his children, including coaching all of their sporting activities. However, one thing I firmly believe is, our thoughts often become our reality. If I chose to look at our new situation as being difficult, then, it would be. I am not naive or unrealistic.

We have definitely had our moments over the past two years. However, I choose to look at my son as my greatest gift and I am so thankful that I have him. I told my son that it was just the two of us now and things could be difficult or they could be good. We have a choice. I remind him of that periodically when we have our difficult moments. I recognize that it is very difficult for him as well. We have both had to make a lot of adjustments. I think my son has been a healing source to me. For the first several weeks after my husband's death, I had no will to live. My only escape from pain was to sleep at night. But each morning, all I had to do was look down the hall at my son's bedroom and I knew I had to get up and carry on because my son desperately needed/ deserved a sense of normalcy in his life. My son was my only inspiration in the early days. I have observed so many changes in him in the last couple of years. Children seem to be so much more resilient than adults. He has assumed much more responsibility around the house and seems to take a sense of pride in handling certain tasks/issues; for example, cleaning the garage, doing little fix-it items, etc. I think it has been healing for him to assume some of the tasks/chores that his dad formerly took care of.

~Michelle G.

As a father, I get pity at school from the mothers and probably everyone else who knows me, especially women. Is this made worse because I have girls?

~Carl L.

I am a father. I feel excluded as all of the mothers gather and I feel out of sorts when I am included. I just don't want this. And I really think I have never even really been a "Man's man!"

~Bruce C.

Lots of people (again nearly all women when I think about it) tell me how well I am doing. They say that they admire and respect what I am doing because I have tailored my life jobs around my kids. I mean, what do they expect me to have done? Send my kids to school in dirty clothes? I wonder if they'd have said the same thing to my wife if it were me that had died? It irks me a bit sometimes. But, if I were completely honest, I'd say that I'm glad that they say it and I even want more people to say it. God it's hard! Before, my wife used to support me in everything I did that was tough or hard. "Good for you." Now there is no one like that in my life. I miss her terribly.

~Bob G.

Even though we're happy and I strive to make life normal, it never will be. How can a dad provide even a partial substitute for a mother's soft and strong love? On Wednesday, as we pulled up on the driveway, my younger daughter said that she had been sad today on the grass at school. She wanted Mommy. My older daughter chipped in and said that she had been sad today as well. (Everyone had been singing the Rugrats song about "I want a Mommy.") I said that I had missed Mom today as well. Then my little one said that it was better with a Mommy and a Daddy. We all agreed.

~Scott M.

Oh, I cried on Thursday night. Not because she was sick but because despite having a high fever, she was still as active and playing happily with her toys and just calling "Papa" when she saw her father's photographs. In addition, she was just walking around the room in circles. She is really walking now! I just cried and cried. I couldn't believe that she's growing up. Her father would miss all this! I can't imagine...it was hard to accept. She really looked so cute and proud as if she had achieved something big. Walking! She is better today, I hope.

~Marion M.

It's about three weeks now that I am managing my daughter alone. If she isn't sick, it's easy for me because she is an obedient and smart child. For the past two weeks, she was sick. With this chronic cough, she has easily thrown up her milk. I found myself washing the bed sheet again and cleaning the mess again. I thank God that He gave me the patience and love not to scold her but to pacify her because she was scared after she vomited. It's the trying times like these when I wish I had an extra pair of hands from my husband. I don't want anyone else. My daughter gets so clingy now, especially because she just turned one year old. I have so little time for myself. I play with her constantly. With my husband around, he would watch over her while I washed the dishes, put the clothes in the machine or even took a shower. Everything I do now must be done in a jiffy. I am getting used to this but at times, I feel the mental strain on me after she sleeps. I have learned to just leave whatever has to be done until later and tend to my daughter first. Although it isn't really my nature to leave things, I have to because I need to be next to her. Another thing that I have learned to do is pre-empt what must be done before she wakes up or before the next morning. I found this keeps me organized and less anxious the following day. Because I am alone now, I need help with parenting. So I have decided to read about parenting in different books.

~Sherry Q.

I've been thinking a bit about a man's perspective. It's interesting. When all of the Mums drop their kids off at school, they have been super sympathetic. This makes me feel somewhat uncomfortable. I was even asked to come along to their monthly drink at the pub! Me and 15 Mums! Blimey! Suffice to say I was (became) busy! I've often thought about how people would have reacted to my wife if it was me that had died. I think there would not have been this great sympathy, especially regarding the kids. Perhaps this is a bit sexist. Probably not, it's just people want to help. One of the things I find most difficult (perhaps as a man, I'm not so sure) is accepting loads of help. I must let other people do their bit. I think it helps their grieving. It helps them get through and it helps you get through.

~Charles M.

When I learned my husband had been killed, I thought of my children. My son had just started school and idolized his father. My husband worked with earth-moving equipment and from the time our son was two, he could name every machine he saw as we drove past road works or building sites. The kids were our life. We had reached the pinnacle of our relationship when we had our first child and they were all we really talked about. My husband had given up a budding music career with a band because our daughter got very sick at five weeks of age. I cried for what my children were going to miss. I had been with him for 15 years and knew everything about him that I could. I had seen the beautiful, the guilty, the sensitive and the selfish. We had laughed, cried, fought and loved each other with such a deep passion that sometimes it hurt. All of the amazing things that made him who he was my children would never see. Photos don't show the soul of a man. You can only see that in a person over many years. They would never know their daddy. The anniversaries of his death were only hard if they landed on one of the kids' birthdays. Christmas was one of those days that I cried my eyes out. I think when you have kids, you have to try so much harder to be strong and brave that you close yourself up. Sadly, I think I also closed myself off to my kids and forgot that they were grieving as well.

~Caren R.

Our adult children have lives of their own. We can't count on them to fill the void. We had our lives at their age and they are entitled to have theirs.

~Susan H.

The saddest thing for me when I look back on that night is how unable I was to care for my children. We collapsed in our separate bundle of agony. We didn't even hug each other. I couldn't bear their pain and they couldn't bear mine. We were lost deep within ourselves. I am so grateful for the family and friends who came to us that night. They cared for my daughter and son. I couldn't even say to my own children that everything was going to be all right. Isn't that terrible? I don't think I ever thought it would be like this. I just don't know.

~Judy L.

When you divorce, the other partner is always still there, somewhere, to pick up the pieces if you fall. By fall, I mean get sick or need some time out. Usually, they take the kids on weekends. Well, imagine this. Suddenly, you are the only person in the whole world fully responsible for three children. Oh yeah, sure, Grandmas and Grandpas are around. No, they did not sire these kids, I did. I have got to say, I used to be a party animal, over indulged regularly on weekends in alcohol and other illegal substances, and for 12 months after my husband died, continued to do it, not caring or thinking.

One day, though, I snapped as I came down from something I shouldn't have taken. I cried, screamed and wondered, "What the hell am I thinking of?" Two weeks later, I jumped on a plane alone and spent three nights at Surfers Paradise. It was a turning point. I realized then that if I died, who would look after my kids and who could take all three and where have I been for nearly 12 months when my kids needed so desperately to have a mum? I was recovering from hangovers for a good part of it. Sure, it helps that I met someone, so I don't need to go out and rage anymore. But even if I hadn't, I really think I would have stopped my insane behavior. I had to because I was the only person in the whole world responsible for my three kids.

~Marcy I.

Without my husband, my parents and grandparents are trying to help. The problem is, we all have different values including what time my child should go to sleep. The family doesn't follow a routine. This is so difficult. They just don't understand. Sometimes, too much help spoils the broth.

~Linda M.

I am a bit worried about my youngest daughter. She doesn't ever mention her mother being gone or even seem concerned. The only thing she has said is that a couple of times she has felt sad. She has also said that she sometimes feels like her mum is still in the Hospice.

While we were riding in the car today, I assured her that it doesn't matter if she gets upset or makes me upset, it's all natural. The latter seemed important to her. She told me that she often looks at clouds in the sky trying to find the whitest one that she thinks her mum lives on. It had to be a nice shape because her mum was always smiling. She pointed out one, which was like her mum going for a run.

At home, while we were snuggling down, I let her know that what she thinks isn't bad and she shouldn't feel guilty. Sometimes, I told her, we have to uncork the bottles and let the air out or it can fester inside. She said, "Is Mum really dead?" She sometimes thinks that her mum may have gone away on a holiday to get better and I have not said anything because it will be a long time. Sadly, I assured her that she was dead and we'd never see her again and that I find it hard to believe sometimes. I told her I had seen Mum's dead body. She asked what it was like.

My daughter also said that she didn't want a memory box. She thought it would be boring. I said that we'd just collect a few things and she was much happier with that.

My daughter also said that there are other things that she has thought. She couldn't remember exactly what now but she would talk in the future. It felt good that we talked, especially about taking corks out.

Later, in the car while we were driving, I asked her if she had five minutes with Mum, what would she say or do with her? My daughter said that she would hug her and tell her she loved her. And they'd go to the park.

My other daughter said that she'd go to the beach with her mum and they would canter on horses at the water's edge.

I hope none of this screws them up...

~Arthur R.

Because my husband was such a hands-on father, this is the greatest loss for me and my child. I could cry buckets if I think of it negatively. On the positive note, I am thankful that I have two great sisters and they are like "sisters" to my child. I am a mom in my twenties. My young friends who have been through parenthood single handedly told me a father always affirms a mother's decision and in this area, I will be lacking. But if I raise my child up in the ways of the Lord, I believe that all things will fall into place. It might sound plain and simple but I want to believe that my child is sensible and understanding.

~Sharlene Q.

My daughter attends a playgroup every Sunday morning. She enjoys it and mingles well and it's a great source of socializing for her. I always brace myself when we go because I have to face so many intact families. I find myself just staring at how a father handles his child or how a couple interacts with their child. I know I have to learn to cope as a single parent and it's very painful at times.

~Jamie K.

The first night I found myself alone in the house, I remember being so scared that I bundled the three children, who I hated in my bed, and I hugged them so tight. I had bought a TV for my bedroom that day. You know, it's the kind with the sleep timer. I needed noise. It really wasn't that bad walking through the house because it was a house that I was used to and it was on a busy street so I was never afraid there.

Five months after my husband's death, I moved to a quiet street in a new area. I was terrified. Every noise was huge and I was convinced that someone was going to break in. I still, after 12 months, have trouble with the silence.

My husband had never been one to jump out of bed at a noise. He never once heard one of our three kid's cry out at night. He would get up if I was scared, though, and he could usually tell the difference between scared and curious.

Funny, how when you think about it, I probably am no more scared of the night now than before. It's just that he's not here to check out the noise so I do it myself.

I have learned to do a lot for myself. I never thought I would or for that matter that I could, but we're survivors. Women with children, watch out world. We are capable of anything to save our "family."

~Marsha A.

Part VII

What I Know For Sure

"What I Know For Sure"

Every month, Oprah writes an article in her magazine entitled, "What I Know For Sure." I read her magazine religiously and I've always admired that she is so certain about what she knows for sure. When I receive her magazine, I flip to this article and I marvel at her ability to have that "knowing." I never thought that I could really know something "for sure" so deep in my soul that no one could change my way of thinking. But after six years of widowhood, I do know some things for sure.

I know for sure that the pain of losing someone you love so deeply never really goes away. I know for sure that we grow a scab over our heart and the scab gets ripped off at different times, leaving us to bleed again even though no one can see the blood. The sheets remain clean as we lay on our beds feeling as if we are dying inside. It's hard to share our pain with others because others have moved on with their lives. They don't know years later, we still bleed on the anniversary of the death, the birthdays, and special occasions like the birth of a grandchild.

What I know for sure is that as time goes on, if we work hard enough, the scab grows back and we move through it faster. I know that no matter how happy we are now, no matter how fortunate we may feel, there are moments that come back and the pain is real. I have made peace with the pain. I know for sure that it will leave. I know for sure that I have it because what I had with my husband was that good. I know that I loved him big time and I hurt big time. I know that I can manage the pain now and have joy again. Joy, that is, differently.

I know for sure that joy is not free. Joy is something that we must work for. After the death of a loved one, we must make joy a goal and work for it. Little by little, the joyful events pile up. Sometime down the road, without realizing it and the timeline is different for everyone, we do have joy again. But comparing the joy we have now to the joy before will prevent real joy from happening. We are not the same now. The joy cannot be the same. But the joy is good...just different.

What I know for sure, really for sure, is that after losing my husband, I lost my innocence. I always knew to live each day in the moment but I realize now that I didn't. Now I know for sure to live each day because there are no guarantees and comparisons don't work. I miss my innocence of safety and "forever," and I'm reminded of it on occasion. Sometimes when I get sad, it's the innocence that I mourn for.

What I know for sure, and I really do know this for sure, is that we can love again. We are not the same because this tragedy has changed us. We are different now and we need a different kind of partner. That's one reason comparisons don't work. This doesn't mean that the new relationship isn't quality. And having a new relationship that makes us happy doesn't mean that we didn't love truly before. What I know for sure is we can love differently and just as much. It's how we look at it. What I know for sure is that it is up to me to reframe how I see things.

Yes, it happened to me 4 1/2 years into widowhood. I have a good, solid relationship with a wonderful man. I never thought that it could happen. I never thought that I could find love at a level that made me really happy again. How could I be lucky twice?

However, it is a very different relationship. Even though I feel fortunate and content, sometimes I have a difficult time being really happy. It's a gray cloud feeling that comes over me. I acknowledge the gray cloud, feel the pain and work hard to go back to joy.

I must remember that it is not a betrayal of my love for my husband if I laugh again and feel love again in a new relationship. The length and depth of my grief cannot be measured by my laughter. I also know that grief will never totally disappear. I work at staying in the moment. I appreciate everything and especially this wonderful man who I look at as a precious treasure.

And what I know for sure is that I live each day of this relationship the best I can. I no longer believe in forever. I know to make a new "normal." I know for sure that this is a new chapter in my life.

To reach Laurie-Ann Weis, please write or e-mail to her at:

Laurie-Ann Weis
30251 Golden Lantern Suite E184
Laguna Niguel, CA 92677-5993
United States of America

E-mail: laurieann@laurieannweis.com

Website: www.laurieannweis.com
(to visit or/and order book by mail)

Telephone: Trafford Publishing 1-888-232-4444
(order book by phone)

Lightning Source UK Ltd.
Milton Keynes UK
21 April 2010

153154UK00001B/63/A

9 781412 066709